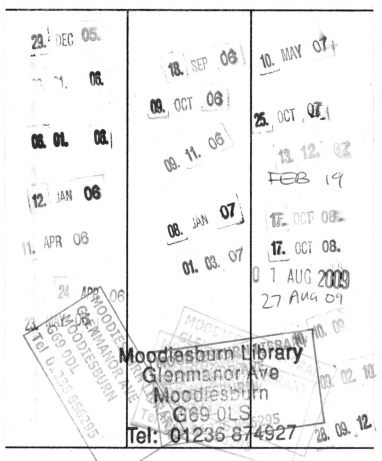

Little Survivors

Little
Survivors

WENSLEY
CLARKSON

JB

JOHN BLAKE

Published by John Blake Publishing Ltd,
3, Bramber Court, 2 Bramber Road,
London W14 9PB, England

www.blake.co.uk

First published in hardback in 2005

ISBN 1 84454 170 3

British Library Cataloguing-in-Publication Data:

A catalogue record for this book is available from the British Library.

Design by www.envydesign.co.uk

Printed in Great Britain by William Clowes Ltd, Beccles, Suffolk

1 3 5 7 9 10 8 6 4 2

Papers used by John Blake Publishing are natural, recyclable products
made from wood grown in sustainable forests. The manufacturing processes
conform to the environmental regulations of the country of origin.

About the author

Wensley Clarkson's experiences as an investigative journalist and author helped him locate the people interviewed for this book. Clarkson's most recent bestseller, *Mother Dearest*, told the extraordinary real-life story of a mother who murdered her two teenage daughters. He has written numerous other non-fiction books, which have sold more than a million copies in 18 countries worldwide.

To all those who didn't make it

Cruelty is a tyrant that is always attended by fear

ENGLISH PROVERB

Contents

INTRODUCTION   xi

1   GALE   1

2   DERMOT   33

3   JANEY   47

4   JOHN   79

5   ANITA   103

6   GRAHAM   129

7   GINNY   153

8   JIMMY   171

9   JENNY   183

10 MARIE   197

Introduction

THIS BOOK IS the result of many voices who have all suffered childhood abuse. My main task was to track down these inspiring people and ensure that their accounts made it into the pages of this book. Each story exposes childhood abuse that all of us can relate to. For, as I discovered, the deeper one goes into such disturbed events, the more complicated those experiences become. I've given the victims themselves the ultimate say in this project and their stories reflect that courageous attitude.

Some of these cases still feature real names because, much to my own surprise, the subjects insisted they had nothing to hide. However, I have changed the names of other individuals who requested anonymity because some of their family members still don't know the truth about their appalling experiences.

I owe a great debt to Rita Wright, a behavioural therapist who kindly introduced me to many of the case histories recalled in this book. Without Rita, *Little Survivors* would not have been possible.

The aim of this book is not to shock and horrify readers but to let you know that even the harshest childhood can be overcome and turned into a positive ingredient in later life. All the people who've told their stories here are the ultimate survivors. They are a testament to the strength of the human spirit.

Wensley Clarkson
2005

1

Gale

IT'S ONLY WHEN I look back at my childhood that I realise what was going on with my parents and how certain incidents helped shape my life. They certainly made the Sopranos look tame in comparison! Yet, to me, my dad always seemed the gentlest father on the planet. But, as I think about what happened, there are images in my head of the comings and goings. It was like a jigsaw and all the pieces have only started fitting together recently.

Mum's best friend – who I always knew as 'Auntie Katie' – owned this tiny little club in Mayfair. When I was a little girl, I'd spend afternoons there with Mum, parading around the club in Auntie Katie's high heels and mink coat. I'd never questioned or even thought about what that club was used for.

Later, my mum told me it was actually a pick-up joint for prostitutes.

Then there were all those bizarre characters with strange nicknames who inhabited my parents' world. Most of them always had great big wads of cash on them. Where did they get all that money from? I used to wonder when I was a child but I never actually asked them.

My mum Doris was a lot different from other parents. She'd been born into a theatrical family in Pimlico, near the Houses of Parliament. Mum was the most beautiful child and everyone told her this, which made her extremely self-centred, spoiled and expectant of others. Her mum – a pianist – died when she was just six years old, so she never really knew what it was like to have a loving mother. When Mum and her siblings were introduced to their new stepmother, she slapped them within minutes of their first meeting.

Mum ran away from home at an early age when her father also started beating her up. No wonder she ended up selling her body in the dodgy back streets of the West End.

My dad, Harry Nelson, came out of Islington, north London, and he'd be nearly 100 years old if he was alive today. Back when he was a teenager, you only escaped from the slums of Islington by joining the army, becoming a villain or in a wooden box. Dad's father died when he was 16, so he eventually left his three brothers, moved up to the West End and started ducking and diving.

Dad began his criminal career in the early 1930s as a hustler in snooker halls. Then he was sent to prison for manslaughter after killing a man, but he never actually told me any more details about what happened. When Dad got out of jail, he bought two nightclubs in Wardour Street in the heart of sleazy Soho – I suppose you'd call them clip joints – which is where he met Mum.

She'd just broken up with another man and was drowning her sorrows there one night. Dad was worried because he'd met her before and she didn't usually drink. Dad's club had prostitutes in it so maybe she was working as a call girl for my dad, who knows? Maybe he *owned* her in every sense of the word. Maybe he was her pimp. So many questions, so few answers.

Dad was six foot tall with dark hair and weighed in at about 16 stone. He was a big guy with big bones. Mum was a size 10 to 12, and she looked Spanish with olive skin and full lips and bore an uncanny resemblance to Bianca Jagger. Back then, they called her exotic. If she walked in a room, everyone would stare at her. They were certainly quite a glamorous couple.

Dad was about 40 when I was born in 1948, which was quite old to be a father back then but the war had got in the way of his family after my brother Michael was born in 1941. The clubs he'd owned in Wardour Street before the war were wiped out by Hitler's bombs, so he'd had to start all over again. But Dad was a grafter and he never stayed still for long. He made a packet during the war running some very lucrative black-market operations.

Dad was a natural born leader but he was also quite a loner who hardly ever went in pubs. My parents' world before I was born consisted more of going with groups of other rich villains to dance at glamorous places like the Ritz, the Waldorf and the Savoy.

When I was born, we lived in the north London suburb of Edgware. Dad had come out of the war a rich man thanks to all those scams and cons he'd been running in the West End. But Mum insisted Dad gave up being a criminal when she became pregnant with me. She'd had enough of all that ducking and diving. She told me she wanted a quiet life after being what these days would be called a 'wild child'.

Mum knew all about the life of a criminal. There was the booze, the other women, the aggro with the police. Men like my dad were hardly ever at home. They were either out thieving, whoring or scamming. Dad's best friend was a little Jewish fella from the East End I knew as 'Uncle Alfie', who was later involved in some of the most notorious London underworld killings in the 1950s. He and Dad were partners in crime in every sense of the word.

Dad's other mates included characters with names like 'Manchester Freddie' and 'Slim Johnson'. But, as I said, he was forced by Mum to give it all up after I was born. Dad even did one last job – I think it was a robbery – and then used all the money to buy two restaurants on the Isle of Sheppey, in Kent, a very popular resort for Londoners back in the 1950s. Mum was determined to get Dad away from all those bad influences in Islington and the West End. They were soon very busy with the restaurants and I was farmed out to nannies and friends while they managed the business.

When I was two, Mum got TB and had to be taken into a hospice. Rather than send me and my brother to foster parents, my father paid for private nannies in the hope Mum would eventually recover. Mum was away for two years in all with TB, which in those days was treated almost like a form of leprosy. Immediately after Mum recovered, my brother said he didn't want to live with us. So she found him a foster mum when she was talking to a woman while queuing up to take some of her earnings from prostitution out of a post office in Mayfair. This lady told Mum about a woman she knew who'd lost her husband but would happily look after one or two children. In some ways, my brother was the lucky one. Dad didn't have the heart to drag him home and he knew Mum was no good at mothering, so he agreed not to take Michael back, although I think it broke his heart.

Back with my parents after Mum's TB scare, they decided when I was just four years old to send me to boarding school. I should have been upset but, as a virtual single child, I longed for the company of other children so I welcomed the move.

The plain, hard truth of the matter was that Mum – who'd run off to the West End at 16 – just didn't know how to be a proper mother. She'd never even done any housework because she'd had a maid since starting work as a call girl. When I was home from school, I was Dad's little blue-eyed girl. I went everywhere I could with him and adored his company. We laughed and joked all the time and I was the apple of his eye. Meanwhile, Mum was cunning, manipulative, immoral and highly sexed. But more about that later.

As a small child, I often wondered why we seemed so rich compared with all our other family members. We had the flash cars, the nannies, the private schools and no one else seemed to have a penny to spare. We were so rich back in those days that Dad often used to hire a chef to make us dinner at home. Most people presumed that having so much money was a godsend but it definitely didn't make my childhood any happier. There are memories that I never thought I'd ever share with anyone, but now I realise how important it is to open up in the hope that it might make parents think about how they can affect the lives of their children.

I first saw the other side of Dad when I went with him in his big American Buick to a place called Leysdown, near Sheppey. It was next to the sea and I remember there were lots of chalets and caravan sites. Anyway, he drove up to this clubhouse with me in the back of his limo. Then he turned to me and said, 'I won't be a minute, darlin'. You stay in the car and don't move.'

I happily replied 'OK' to whatever Dad said back in those days. He was my hero in every sense of the word.

So Dad went into this clubhouse. A few minutes later, he walked back out briskly and got into the Buick, started it up and gently revved the engine.

'You all right, babe?' he asked me, as I sat quietly in the back of the car.

'Yes, Daddy.'

Just then, a man came out of the premises. Dad's car then rolled forwards. This man was just in front of us.

I felt the bonnet surge upwards, as Dad pressed down hard on the accelerator. Suddenly, there was a thud as Dad's car bonnet hit the man and he flew up into the air before falling to the ground.

Dad then slammed the brakes on before cranking the car into reverse and backed right over this man as he lay there. I remember looking up at the rear-view mirror and seeing Dad's steely-blue eyes staring straight ahead, even though the car had just reversed over that 'bump'. Then he caught me a glance and his eyes changed shape as he smiled a broad grin in my direction. I didn't even bother to try to look out of the window to see what had happened to the man. Later on, I thought that maybe the man we'd run over was one of the fellas always chasing Mum.

Anyway, the rest of the day went off without incident and, naturally, Dad's 'driving skills' were never mentioned again. I never really thought about the true significance of that incident until many years later. This was my dad at work and I don't know to this day if that man lived or died in that car park. At the time, I just knew it was none of my business.

Not long afterwards, Mum got this parcel in the post and it contained someone's ear. I can laugh about it now, but it was pretty horrific at the time. All I can remember her saying was: 'I don't know if this is from yer fuckin' father or Uncle Alfie or one of their lot. But it's completely out of order.'

She wasn't scared – just irritated. I still don't even know if she ever asked my Dad what it was all about.

So the threat of violence was omnipresent. Many things in my childhood were affected by it and I became so aware of my father's attachment to violence that I feared an explosion from him at any moment. One time, when I was about 11 or 12, I was playing handstands on a wall near our home and there was this bloke nearby who kept staring at us. My cousin Kay – who had come to stay with us – whispered to me, 'That bloke's looking up our knickers.'

I responded, 'Don't tell Dad,' because I didn't want this man to end up dead.

But she ignored me and insisted, 'I'm gonna go and tell Uncle Harry.'

I repeated, 'Please don't tell my dad, whatever you do.'

But Kay ran straight into our restaurant and said, 'Uncle Harry, there's a bloke out there and he's looking up our skirts.'

We were immediately ushered into the house. An old boyfriend of mine later told me that Dad then went out to see the man. The story goes that Dad killed that man and had him buried in a nearby graveyard. Whatever the man did, he didn't deserve to pay for it with his life but I'll bet in Dad's mind he was just being protective.

With all these pressures on them, I suppose it's no surprise that my parents argued all the time. But I loved them both, whatever they put me through. I'd always stick up for them. 'At least they paid the bills,' I told my brother Michael once many years ago.

My brother coped with the way my parents were by isolating himself and not allowing anyone into his own little world. I coped by over-caring for both my parents. I was ready to drop everything to make sure I kept the peace between them.

My parents were both very flamboyant and I don't think they could really be arsed to look after their children most of the time. But they always seemed happy to help other people out. The whole family got money off Mum and Dad. I now realise it was a classic criminal thing. You always shared your money with others less fortunate. It's called looking after your own.

Often when Mum and Dad argued, it sounded as if he was trying to shut her up in case she blurted something out about him. He must have had so many secrets that she could have landed him right in it.

But when I was small, they kept sending us away. Here I was, Daddy's blue-eyed girl, yet he was constantly trying to get rid of me. It didn't seem fair.

My brother's banishment was a good result for him because at least he was in a happy environment. I never experienced that. Neglect is a form of abuse. So, much of the time it felt as if I was raising myself.

Holidays were about the only times when we were all properly together. We went all over Europe. Dad would hire a Vauxhall Cresta convertible or we'd go in one of his American gas-guzzlers. Christmas was also pleasant because there were no arguments and lots of presents. It was also the only time Mum was allowed to cook properly. She used to wind Dad up by always bringing someone poor in off the street for Christmas dinner. She was incredibly generous and had no appreciation of money. We had our own accounts at Selfridges, Harrods and Hamleys as well as at all the local shops. And Mum was always giving money away to assorted friends and relatives.

Neither of my parents drank a lot. Dad had loved whisky up until I was born but it sent him so crazy he hardly touched it after I came on the scene. He was very controlling, which was why he drank so little. He once said he didn't trust himself when he was drunk. I heard he was extremely violent on whisky and that was why he ended up in prison for manslaughter before the war.

Going to a posh boarding school provided me with an escape from a miserable home life. I couldn't understand why my brother Michael didn't like boarding school. I adored it. The teachers and pupils became like my real family and provided an important structure in my life.

I used to see Mum and Dad when they came down to school in his expensive Cadillac or the Buick. It was this really big manor house with a huge oak staircase, and when parents arrived the headmistress would lead us down this staircase to meet them. I had this velvet-collared overcoat with hat and gloves and I'd walk down the stairs and there would be Mum in her fox-fur wrap and Dad in his crombie and polished brogues. They'd then take me off to the Dreamland amusement park in nearby Margate for the weekend. The school eventually stopped allowing me to go off with them for weekends because there were a lot of diplomats' children there. Their parents couldn't come at weekends and it was upsetting the other pupils that I was able to go off to Dreamland for a whole weekend and they couldn't.

I was well liked at boarding school because I had the best tuck boxes and seemed to have the most charmed life. Back then, I remember thinking Dad worked as the manager of a shoe factory because at one time he did own a shoe factory, although I later learned he got it as part of a gambling debt from another criminal.

I was terribly disappointed when they took me out of boarding school at the age of eight, although Dad agreed to send me to a private day school called Airedale, on the Isle of Sheppey. That's when Mum's promiscuity caught up with us. A lot of the other girls at this new school started bullying me. Mum was branded 'a slag' by some of them because she'd become the talk of the island. She'd started sleeping with other men whenever Dad travelled up to London on business. Back in those days, we were one of the richest families on the island. Even now, when I occasionally visit the island, they still think of us that way.

The bullying at school eased off when I started hitting my classmates back if anyone ever said anything rude about Mum. I eventually got quite a fearsome reputation. I even knocked out a couple of girls. One time I had to go to hospital for treatment after yet another fight and Dad asked me what had started it all. I lied and said another girl had been teasing me about my hair. He later admitted to me he was glad I'd punched this girl's face in because that was the way he'd been brought up. The Nelsons always got in first and sorted out people who were trying to push them around.

Even though I was a girl, I was brought up more like a boy. I wasn't feminine and gentle. My family all went on about how I should always remember who I was but, in reality, I didn't really know until years later when I really worked out what Mum and Dad had been up to in the underworld.

Today, I realise that much of the abuse I suffered was a direct result of Mum's affairs. A few times, she even left home and went off with guys knowing full well that if Dad tracked her down he was more than capable of shooting her.

Mum would turn up at the gates of my private school and say, 'Right, we're off.' Her latest boyfriend would be with her and he'd drive us, always in a flashy car. She never explained what was happening. We'd end up in flats in places like Knightsbridge and Kensington with these men. Often we'd disappear for a month or two. I found out later that Dad would be trying to hunt us down. Eventually, he'd catch up with Mum and she'd take me home.

Then one of her lovers sexually abused me when we went to live in his flat in the West End. He crept into my bedroom one night and forced me to do things to him. I was 12 at the time. I never told a soul what happened, especially not Dad. I'd seen Dad attack other people who had crossed him and I knew what he was capable of. I absolutely adored him in many ways but I didn't want to be responsible for him killing another man.

Mum never explained why she kept running off with these other men. Each time she picked me up from school with yet another man, I pleaded to stay with Dad. Even now, I don't really know why she made me go with her the whole time. Maybe she was using me as a pawn to try to wind him up because she knew how much he loved me.

Mum always swore me to secrecy not to tell Dad about her numerous affairs. It was a dreadful pressure to put on a child, and that heavy burden reversed our roles; I became more like the mother than the child. I seemed to be forever covering our tracks so that Dad didn't explode into a murderous rage. But there were occasions when his violence almost seemed to turn Mum on.

One time, we were all at a wedding and Mum was in one of her weird moods. She looked stunningly pretty and every man there seemed interested in her. She loved the attention. Then, after the speeches when everyone was dancing and drinking, she suddenly turned to me and said, 'Watch yer dad. Watch yer dad. He's had a whisky.' Her voice was virtually trembling with excitement. She seemed to be relishing Dad losing it big time with some poor innocent bastard. Then she nudged me. 'Look, I told you. I told you.'

There was Dad just ten feet from us holding this

bloke up by his throat and saying to him, 'You can die now or later, sonny.'

The bloke was shaking with fear as Dad tightened his grip on his neck.

A few moments later, he let the man go and he crumpled to the floor. All the other wedding guests ignored the incident. The man then struggled to his feet and Dad gave him an almighty kick up the backside as he headed for the exit. I don't know what the argument was about, but I presume that this man must have been giving Mum the eye. Anyway, Dad casually brushed down the front of his jacket and came over and joined us. He didn't even look stressed.

Mum was the complete opposite – always very dramatic. When she hit me, she'd also shout and scream and swear in my face. 'I wish you were never born!' was her favourite. This would be followed by 'I hate you.' She had numerous abortions before and after I was born, although she only admitted all this to me many years later.

Mum only really cared about herself. She bought herself beautiful clothes and wore all the best perfume and make-up. I particularly remember her with a black top and her hair swirled around with a flower sticking out, dripping in jewellery. I came a poor third. I remember often thinking how beautiful she was but that I mustn't touch. She was like extremely delicate porcelain – liable to crack at any moment. Throughout my childhood, I don't ever recall her touching me or dressing me or showing me any real affection.

Then, when I was 12, Dad went bankrupt. He lost the restaurants and the house and just about everything else. I remember the day they came and took away his collection of American cars. It broke his heart. Luckily, he'd always kept on this small council flat in Islington so we went back there and restarted our lives. We would have been homeless without it. But it was a council flat with a difference, because it was done up top to bottom with expensive furniture they'd taken before the bailiffs could nick it and it even had plush Wilton carpets.

I had to go to a horrible comprehensive school in nearby Newington Green. I was bullied from the moment I turned up for lessons.

Until then, I'd always called my parents 'Mummy' and 'Daddy'. Now I had to adjust to a different world from the one I had known and it was quite a shock.

Life got much more dangerous for us when Dad went broke. He'd put all the businesses in Mum's name to avoid tax and then she refused to sell up. As a result, he had to get a job as a chauffeur just to make ends meet. It had been perfect for her because while he was up in London she could seduce anyone who caught her eye.

By then, Mum was regularly throwing things at me, pulling my hair and bashing my head against the wall whenever she wanted to make a point. It could be at any time of the day or night. She was incredibly unpredictable. The attacks on me increased after Dad lost all his money and she went on pills called Preladin, which seemed to cause her even bigger mood swings, although they were supposed to give her energy. Afterwards, she'd always beg me not to tell Dad she'd hit me and she was very careful never to hit me in front of him. I'd never tell Dad because that would have been a betrayal. And we Nelsons were always told never to 'grass up yer own' – or anyone else for that matter. I was also worried that Dad would kill her if he knew she'd laid a finger on me.

The flat in Islington was often a complete tip when Dad came home from work and Mum would say I made it like that when it was really her. I'd been out at school all day and she hadn't been out of bed. But, when I got into my teens, I started shouting back. The nearest I got to hitting her was when I threw a plant pot at her just as Dad walked in. Mum encouraged him to pick me up with his huge hands. He then said, if I ever did that to Mum again, we would fall out big time. I was so angry with my mother for forcing him to take sides.

Another time, Dad was on the verge of hitting me after a row and I threatened to call the police. He completely backed down, began laughing hysterically and walked off. But Dad didn't have to hit you to make his point. He just had this look on his face, which was enough. You knew you had to behave.

And in family circles, there was always this whisper about Mum. 'Oooh, you know about Doris, don't you?' some relatives would say. They used to call her 'the wild one'. It wasn't until many years later I fully realised why.

Meanwhile, Dad dipped his toe back in the underworld whenever it suited him. I remember coming home from school one weekend and finding Dad and his mates burning all this stuff in the garden of our ground-floor flat. I must have been aged about 13 and Mum said to me, 'You can't go in the garden. Dad's out there with Uncle Alfie.'

That immediately sparked my curiosity, so I replied, 'What're they doing?'

'They're burning stuff,' was all Mum would say.

So I asked, 'Why?'

Mum just replied, 'Yer dad had to get rid of a car.'

That was it. No other explanation.

So I kept prodding. 'What car?'

It still didn't dawn on me that they were up to no good. But Mum had had enough so she snapped back, 'It doesn't matter. I'm telling you not to go out there.'

She then told me to go in the street and play for a while. Later, there was a big court case involving Dad's mate Uncle Alfie and I realised they had been destroying evidence connecting them to a murder.

Meanwhile, Mum was getting more and more hooked on these so-called uppers called Preladin. One minute she was up in spirits, the next she was down at the bottom of the ladder. It was dreadful for a child to have to cope with. She was all over the place, sometimes spending days on end in bed. Then she'd take out even more of her frustrations on me.

A classic example was when I came in from school one day and she barked out that she wanted me to bring her tea up on a tray. When I got to her bedroom with this tea tray, Mum screamed at me, 'You haven't fuckin' laid the tray properly!' Then she threw the tray over my head. At that moment, my brother Michael – who was visiting us – rushed in and grabbed Mum by the throat and screamed at her, 'If you ever do that to her again, I'll have you!'

I have a distinct memory of that particular incident because at the time I kept thinking it was all my fault. If I'd done the tea properly, she would never have thrown the tray at me. And I continued presuming that her behaviour was no different from other mothers.

Mum would also secretly order me to go out and get her precious pills from a local bookie, who was also a drug dealer. I'd get them and slip them to her out of Dad's sight. Then he'd pull me the other way by yelling at me, 'Your mother's been taking those pills, hasn't she?'

I'd simply respond, 'Has she?'

Then he'd say, 'Where's she gettin' them from?'

I'd reply, 'I dunno.'

When I reached puberty, I became an even more unhappy child as all that frustration and repression kicked in. I'd have massive tantrums and smash things up. I had a horrendous temper. People used to say I filled a room with fear whenever I walked in. Others called it 'a touch of the Nelsons'. It was a form of madness because you don't know what you're doing when you lose it and I suspect Dad flipped out just like that as well. Mum had a temper but it wasn't in the same league as Dad's, even though he kept the lid on it most of the time. But sometimes he'd get Mum by the throat up against a wall and I'd have to break them up because I was the only one who could actually pacify Dad. Mum just kept winding him up. It got so bad at one stage that, if Mum wanted something from Dad, she'd ask me to get it for her, rather than risk a beating or a throttling. I'd become the ultimate piggy in the middle.

Mum and Dad both gradually began to withdraw from the rich, glamorous lifestyle they'd been used to. Back in that small council flat they became more dependent on each other.

The most dangerous rows between them came when she'd throw something at him and he'd completely lose it. I don't remember ever seeing Mum with a black eye or bruises or anything so I think he must have been very careful not to mark her. But Dad had these massive hands and I often saw him pick her up by the throat and throw her through the air. Then she'd hit the floor with a thump and start crying out for me because she knew I was the only one who could stop him going completely crazy.

I'd run into the room and scream out, 'Dad, Dad, stop it!' Usually that would make him come to his senses but he never said sorry about hitting my mother.

But the family still always came first. Dad even 'adopted' a few lost souls, including the father of a notorious north London gang of brothers and helped him get on his feet. They were eternally grateful to Dad and sent him money until the day he died.

Despite Dad's close involvement in crime, I never

saw guns in the house, although I'm pretty sure there had been some around. Plain-clothes detectives occasionally turned up at the front door. Dad and his mates even had this code whereby, if someone was arrested, no one else would speak to them on the phone 'in case others were listening in'.

Then, one day, Mum landed me in it by moaning to Dad about me not doing the housework. He believed her and turned on me and said I was out of order. I was flabbergasted by Mum's lies.

'What you talking about? I've been doing everything,' I responded.

Then Dad steamed in. 'If you don't like it, then get out.'

I was infuriated. 'OK, I'm off.'

I walked out minutes later. I was as stubborn as my father.

At the time, I was going out with a boy called Barry. He lived in Hackney so I headed there and Barry's mum let me stay at the family home for a bit, and then Barry's aunt Val rented me a room in her house around the corner in Douglas Square, Hackney. It cost a couple of quid a week and was right next to the bathroom so the other eight inhabitants of the house walked past my room constantly. There was an Irish pair at the top who used to have a fight every week and kick each other down the stairs.

I never saw either Mum or Dad again for a year. Not a word or a phone call – nothing. They never found out where I was. These days I would have been called a missing person but back then no one seemed to care.

I got myself a job as a machinist in a factory. Then, a year after moving out, I was walking down Ridley Road market and I bumped into Mum and Dad, which was pretty strange. We were very civil to each other and Dad looked so relieved to have found me. He even asked me if I'd come home but I refused. Typically, both of them then went a bit over the top. They came and saw the room and insisted on having it properly decorated and carpeted. I gave them a key and let them get on with it.

Mum seemed fine about me living away from home. I soon found out why. One day, I came back from work and my landlady Val said she needed a word with me. I could tell it was serious from the tone of her voice. She told me Mum was letting herself in with that spare key and having sex with men in my room. She'd only had it done up so she could turn it into a knocking shop.

I confronted Mum and all she could say was, 'I never meant any harm. I didn't think you'd find out.'

'If you ever do it again, I'll tell Dad,' I said. 'You've made me look really bad in front of my boyfriend's family. Thanks.'

'All right, all right. I won't do it again.' She sounded more like a naughty little girl than a parent.

Then I took my key back from her just to make sure. I now knew I could never trust Mum. I presumed the men were lovers but they might have been punters I suppose. But I never told Dad what had happened because I still feared he could kill her. Despite everything, I didn't want to lose her.

I first heard the full truth about my parents during my divorce hearing when I was 26. My ex-husband decided to reveal Mum and Dad's life of crime to show that I was not a fit mother to bring up our child. He failed, but it left me very angry with both of my parents for keeping their secret life from me.

When I walked out of the court that day, I turned to my father and said, 'You'll never guess what my ex said in court, that you were a villain…'

Dad interrupted: 'I think we need to talk.'

I continued: '… and listen to this one, Mum was a call girl.'

Dad repeated, 'We need to talk.'

Anyway, we talked in the corridor of that court in the Strand and he came clean. 'It's all true. I was a villain. I've also been inside and done time for manslaughter. And your mum was a call girl when I first met her.' That took a lot of guts especially since Dad was chauffeuring by this time. At first, I was really shocked and wondered how I would get my head around what my parents had been in their former life. Dad's way of thinking was that he wanted us to have the life he'd never had by sending us to an expensive boarding school, living in a big mansion and enjoying life's luxuries.

That afternoon, we went home together from the court and began discussing everything in even more detail. Mum then joined in and admitted, 'I never expected to have to tell you about us.' Mum even mentioned all these lords and other high-class people who used to go Auntie Katie's club. We sat and talked for hours. It was a magical time because the veil of lies had been lifted and suddenly all those past tensions disappeared.

Dad even explained the whole criminal world of apprenticeships and how it worked. How certain chosen characters were carefully trained in the art of criminality. The pecking order and who took orders from whom.

Dad said he first got pulled into the underworld when he was a teenager and went to a dance where there was a fight with knives that ended in victory for Dad and his brothers. That got the Nelsons a reputation on the manor as a really hard family.

People stood back and respected Dad especially. No one wanted any aggro with him or his clan.

I then decided it was finally time to tell Mum how one of her lovers had sexually abused me when we all lived in that apartment in Knightsbridge. She was horrified. The following day – so she told me years later when she was about to die – she went down to the Isle of Sheppey where she'd first met this man and tracked him down. She found him and glassed him in a pub. Dad would have killed him if he'd known what had happened.

I ran into an ex-boyfriend from the Isle of Sheppey some time later and I asked him what had really happened to that man and he said, 'The only thing I know is that your mum glassed him in his face.' So she'd been telling the truth. Even my mum was capable of caring about me, although it was a pretty twisted reaction.

But there were other disturbing secrets that only began to emerge after I fully understood my parents' criminal connections. A long time before Mum's death, I found out from her that she'd been to bed with Dad's best mate, 'Uncle Alfie'. She let it slip after we had a huge row. I was so angry about it, but she begged me not to tell Dad. I saw this as a bigger betrayal than any of her other affairs. This time I wasn't so sure I could keep quiet to Dad about it.

Eventually, it all blew up at home one day and everything spilled out. I remember saying to Dad, 'You think Uncle Alfie is your friend? Well, he's been having an affair with Mum.'

Dad went deathly quiet and then charged straight out of the house. I think he had to get out before he exploded. A couple of hours later, he came back and said to both of us, 'As far as I'm concerned, he's dead.'

That was the end of a lifelong friendship. I suppose Alfie should count himself lucky Dad didn't kill him. But Dad kept to his word and never saw him again or even went to Alfie's funeral years later.

But every time Mum did something like this it meant Dad owned her even more. She never seemed to feel any guilt. Sometimes I wondered if she was some kind of nymphomaniac who was simply addicted to sex.

When my own kids were quite young, I went on a holiday to Benidorm in Spain with Mum. She called my youngest son a drip over and over when he was trying to dance in a bar. In the end, I stormed off to a nearby fair with the kids to get away from her, but when I came back she had a right go at me, saying I should never have left her. Then she added, 'I've been such a good mother to you.'

Well, I lost it completely then. I headbutted her and grabbed her by the throat and I think I was close to killing her. Everything came back to me on that day. All she kept saying was: 'You're mental. You've always been mental.'

We never spoke again for over a year. Dad wouldn't speak to me either. Mum was God and he'd taken her side. Funny thing is that, after all that violence between them and that secret life of crime and vice, they were joined at the hip in later life. My friends used to look at them and say, 'I want to be like Harry and Doris. They look like the perfect couple.' Little did they know.

A few years ago, I found an old-fashioned vest in the attic, which had been hand embroidered with a heart on it containing the letters 'D' and 'H'. I asked Mum what it was and she said Dad made it for her when he was briefly banged up in prison again. Maybe they were in love all the time but had a strange way of showing it.

Dad had this extraordinary knack of doing exactly what he said he would do. I don't ever remember him promising me something he couldn't deliver. I think that was a criminal way of thinking and yet it was in some ways an incredibly good way to lead your life. The honour and respect didn't all just lead to violence. There were many good sides to it. Dad's only vice in old age was smoking pungent Bolivar cigars. Whenever I smell them in the air now, it's like he must be watching over me keeping an eye on his beloved daughter.

Then Mum had a heart attack, which was probably caused by all those drugs she'd been taking. It was a big attack and life-threatening. I was in the house when they resuscitated her. She actually stopped breathing for nearly four minutes. But her illness was probably one of the best things that ever happened to my parents' relationship because afterwards Dad turned into her nurse.

They truly couldn't survive without each other. Dad would wash her hair lovingly, get her dressed and everything while she was recovering from that heart attack. He'd finally got her to himself. She stopped falling for other men and seemed satisfied with her life for the first time in her marriage. They settled down into some form of normality, although of course they still controlled each other in different ways.

Dad found it hard to adjust to today's attitudes and values. A classic example was the respect that should be shown by a son to his mother. He'd supported his mum until the day she died and he couldn't understand why my sons weren't like that. But times had changed.

Twelve years ago, when Dad lay on his bed dying of old age, he looked like a version of Marlon Brando in *The Godfather*. I glanced down at his shrunken body and for the first time I saw the criminal within him. He had this aura around him just before he died. It was almost magical. He even whispered gently to my then husband, 'Will you please take care of my daughter?' It was said in such a way that my husband knew that he dared not disobey him. When he died, they did him a full-size snooker table in flowers for the funeral to mark his humble beginnings as a hustler on the tables.

But, even in those long, difficult days before he died, he never once lost his cool. He never shook with rage and in some ways that made him more scary. He had been a truly powerful criminal respected throughout his manor. He didn't need to blow a gasket to make a point. He flicked his fingers and people did what was required. That was real power.

Now that both my parents are dead, I've at last come to terms properly with my childhood and realise that, despite all the horrific incidents and the bizarre world within which Mum and Dad existed, I can take strength from those experiences. They've moulded me into who I am and my character is resilient and strong because of what happened. I am now happily married to an honest, respectable man and living in a beautiful house with a swimming pool and a fantastic lifestyle to match. In a strange sort of way, I would never have got this without the past, so thanks, Mum and Dad. Life would never have been the same without you!

2

Dermot

I WAS BORN just before the last war in a stinking, rundown tenement in Lower Dominic Street, Dublin. Me, my mam and my four brothers and sisters lived out of one room in that four-storey block. The front door to each room opened straight out on to a balcony and you got down to the ground floor by way of a twisting baronial-style staircase, which was completely out of keeping with the rest of the crumbling building. There was no electricity, no toilet and we were lucky if we got a bath once a week at the local municipal pools. There was a field behind the flats that was our crapper – the local farmers reckoned we produced the best fertiliser in Dublin!

My life changed forever the night two black

Humber Hawks drew up outside my home and four of the ugliest, fattest bastard women you ever laid your eyes upon came up to take us away. They were accompanied by Gardai (police) officers. Later, the neighbours said you could hear the screaming and the crying from the other end of the street.

All my older brothers and sisters were huddled together in the one bed they shared in a corner of the room as the footsteps approached. The strangers pulled the kids from their bed and dragged them out. It was like a tug of war. They were fighting and kicking like mad. My mam Marie started saying 'Hail Marys' over and over. Then she began pleading, 'Leave it for now. I changed my mind.'

Mam had actually asked the authorities to take us away because she couldn't cope. She made a few pennies by pushing a pramload of washing around where we lived. But she was a big drinker so those few pennies all went straight down her throat.

Imagine the chaos: nothing but a flickering gas lamp on the mantelpiece illuminated this dreadful scene, as my brothers and sisters were taken away, all because my father was already married with a family on the other side of town.

I only know about what happened that night because I had it described to me years later. I was just eight months old at the time, but that awful event shaped the rest of my life and those of my siblings. As those horrible women virtually knocked the door down and grabbed my brothers and sisters, I remained fast asleep wrapped in a blanket in a big orange box in the corner of the room.

Apparently, that box was pushed over in the melee and I rolled into a pitch-black corner and they completely missed me. Meanwhile, the screams of my brothers and sisters had become so loud that many of the other tenants came from surrounding rooms and tried to attack the sheriff's women and the Gardai officers as they headed down the stairs towards those sinister dark sedans.

They'd wrapped the kids in blankets as they kicked and screamed. The eldest two – John, eight, and Richard, ten – fought like tigers. They screamed. They bit. They just wouldn't give up without a fight. The girls – Geraldine, four, and Patricia, five – were taken out the door first. I guess they were easier to handle. My brothers were left to two hefty Gardai who gave them a right smacking in the process. Meanwhile, my mam was still huddled in the corner of the room, crying her eyes out.

'They're taking my children away,' she screamed in the hope they might stop. She'd changed her mind about having them taken away and it must have been heartbreaking to watch.

Her little girls were crying, 'Mammy! Don't leave us, Mammy. Please don't leave us!'

Mam had asked them to be taken away because our father had refused to support us, his *other* family. He'd long since disappeared. Mam felt she had no choice. It was the only way to ensure the kids got fed. But now she felt nothing but shame because she'd encouraged this 'kidnapping'.

The neighbours formed an arch to try and stop the coppers leaving with the kids so they took out their batons and smashed a route through. Then some of the good residents of Lower Dominic Street threw sticks and bricks at the Gardai to stop them reaching the cars. Some suffered broken fingers as their hands were smashed by batons. One copper had his eyes gashed while he fought with one of our neighbours, a big old lump of a bus driver called Sean O'Connell. But my brothers and sisters were still being dragged down the stairs.

Then my mam ran to the top of the stairs and started yelling after them. 'Don't take 'em! Please don't take 'em. I changed me mind. I'll look after 'em. Please!'

But Mam's plea fell on deaf ears.

Mam caught up with the sheriff's possee as they got down to the ground floor. She grabbed at this woman's hair and then tried to pull my sister Geraldine out of her arms. Just then a Gardai officer smashed a baton down hard on Mam's back. She wasn't strong enough to take on the mighty long arm of the law. The kids were still being dragged towards the cars.

Back in that shitty-smelling, gaslit room, I was crying my eyes out, aged eight months. I'd survived because I'd fallen out of that orange box when they grabbed the others. My mother was in despair because she couldn't handle the guilt she felt.

So later that same night she passed me over to her sister Lia who from that day onwards became my mother. Lia lived upstairs and had come down when she heard the commotion. Lia couldn't have children of her own so she and her husband were delighted to take me. They immediately changed my name and birthday so that no one knew it was me. My name went from John to Dermot and they also changed my date of birth by a couple of months. But they kept the same surname. I never discovered the truth until I applied for a passport many years later.

Lia's husband − I suppose you'd call him my stepfather or adoptive dad − was a notorious street fighter with a fearsome reputation on the streets of Dublin. His name was Jimmy Maguire and he already had plans for my future, but more of that later.

Maguire was a tall, rugged man in his late thirties, handsome with a shock of black curls. Later, he taught me how to write because I hardly ever went to school.

Usually, I'd eat my sandwiches the moment I got there and then head straight home after I'd nicked a few bottles of milk.

Maguire was a very clever man and he decided to train me up as his little thief. He'd show me where to go and what to steal. Maguire was like a Dublin version of Fagin, getting me out on the streets to do his dirty work. He orchestrated everything. One time he got me a Saturday job in a shoe shop and, because he was then working as a dustman, he'd come along with a bin and I used to have to fill it with nicked shoes.

And, if I disobeyed his orders, he'd lay into me. Maguire had this broom he'd start swinging around his head until he eventually caught you with it. Then he'd use the handle to prod you so hard it really hurt and there were always bruises afterwards to prove it. I never called that bastard 'Dad'. Never called him anything in fact, although he called me 'Lightning' because I was so fast on my feet.

One time, Maguire made me traipse around the whole of Dublin to find him a certain moneylender. I went to loads of pubs just to get ten bob for Maguire. I knew, if I failed, I'd get a belting. I eventually tracked the moneylender down and got Maguire his ten shillings. On Fridays, Maguire and Lia would give me sixpence and a list to go shopping. I had to get Yorkshire potatoes, cabbage, Brussels sprouts. I stole it all and spent the sixpence on a few sweets for myself.

Then Lia surprised everyone in the family by getting pregnant – and that's when my life took a turn for the worse. I soon got pushed to one side. After the birth of their son, Lia even started treating me as if I was some kind of rival for Maguire's attention.

By the time I was six years old, Maguire had turned me into a serious thief through a combination of intimidation and good training. He even forced me to systematically rob a little old lady called Mrs Mulchrone who lived next door to us and I still haven't recovered from the guilt it caused me.

Maguire made me go into her room every other day and steal her tea and sugar because we couldn't afford any. I think she suspected that I was doing it but she was so old and frail that she couldn't be bothered to do anything about it.

I always knew when Mrs Mulchrone was in the hallway because she would stand there in that huge coat of hers, pissing on the wooden floor. I could hear the noise in our room and that's when Maguire would say, 'Go and get some tea and sugar, Lightning.'

So I'd slide along the wall behind her and get whatever I could. I remember in her room there was a crucifix on the mantelpiece and it would be looking right at you. I didn't like that one bit.

Then Mrs Mulchrone started carrying everything in

her coat pockets to stop me stealing it and she even put sellotape on her pockets to stop the food falling out. She also had butter as well as the tea and sugar and it often ended up a congealed mess in her pockets.

Then Mrs Mulchrone died. Maguire heard from a neighbour before anyone else and sent me in to nick her cash savings as her corpse lay there in the darkness. She'd been planning to give that money to the Church and Maguire knew she had the cash on her at all times.

Robbing a body that was not yet cold would be a daunting task for anyone, but for a six-year-old it was terrifying. However, I knew if I failed I'd get beaten to within an inch of my own life. I was already the outsider of the family. I still never called Maguire 'Father' or 'Dad' but I suppose I wanted some kind of approval from him so I agreed to rob Mrs Mulchrone's corpse. Maguire told me the money was in a paper bag stuffed down the front of her bodice.

'Before anyone gets here, get what you can, Lightning.' He knew that someone would turn up from the local morgue within a couple of hours. Naturally, Maguire told me not to come back empty-handed or I'd be in for a kicking.

So I crept into that dark, stinking room and found her lying dead on a chair. She was clad only in her dirty, yellowing underwear and her coat, which was wrapped around her shrivelled-up little corpse.

I scrambled around in the dark, barely able to make out the silhouette of her corpse, faintly backlit by candlelight from the mantelpiece. I pulled open the front of her coat and felt the nausea overwhelming me. The bag of money didn't seem to be there so I left the coat hanging open and crept back next door.

Maguire hit the roof when I walked in empty-handed. 'Go back in there and fuckin' get it! You fuckin' tinker cunt!' He always liked to remind me that I was from gypsy stock.

So I went back into the dark passageway and slipped quietly into her room once again. I nearly fell head over heels on her piss and shit that was smeared on the floor. It's difficult to describe the fear I felt. I tried looking beneath her bodice but the smell and texture of her body repulsed me.

So I held my breath and tried to wriggle my hand beneath this bodice she had on. I felt around quickly and was horrified when I realised I'd touched her nipple, but still I failed to find the bag of money.

This time Maguire went crazy and punched me in the back of the head.

'Bollicks! Get back in dere and fuckin' find it, yer little toad. Get that fuckin' money! This is yer last chance. Don't come back without it, yer fuckin' tinker shite bastard,' he yelled at me. Then his eyes flared up with relish as he added, 'Strip her if you have to, but get dat money.'

A couple of minutes later, I shut my eyes and plunged my hand towards her saggy breasts and felt the damp paperbag crumple against my fingertips. I grabbed it and let out a deep breath. I thought I'd be attacked by the Devil himself, especially when I looked at that crucifix staring down at me from the mantelpiece. It was lit up eerily by the streetlamp outside the window.

My heart was beating so fast. As I grabbed the money, I fell and clutched on to something. As I squeezed the clammy flesh, I realised it was her thigh. In my haste to scramble away, I lost my footing and pulled her corpse down on top of me. I thought she'd come alive and got me. I was so scared I scrambled out from under her corpse and slithered out of that room across the piss and the shit. I actually felt my bare feet squidging down on the excrement. I knew that if any got between my toes I wouldn't be allowed back in the Maguires' because of the smell.

But in my haste to get out of Mrs Mulchrone's I slipped again and dropped the money somewhere on the soiled floor. I grappled through the dark and felt through the urine puddles on the bare wood surface. Then I touched a damp cloth that smelled of excrement. Finally, I found the notes next to her rotting feet. By this time I'd wet myself with fear.

Maguire only grunted when I finally delivered the booty. But next day he rewarded me by buying me a suit for my Holy Communion. He was a cruel bastard but he could also be kind.

Mrs Mulchrone soon came back to haunt me. Every time I tried to sleep, an image of her pale, bloated body came into my mind. I kept replaying that awful night when I had to go into her one room.

Meanwhile, Maguire found new excuses to beat me. I'd get whacked for daring to ask for some pudding when my stepmother – or rather my aunt – Lia had eaten the whole lot before I got home. Lia would make out I'd been rude to her and he'd steam in very hard.

Lia had become a greedy, fat woman by this time. There was hardly ever a morsel of food left for me. One time, when I was about ten, I was so upset I stormed out of the room and ran down to the small farmyard at the back of our block. I was in a fury. I felt so unloved and uncared for. I hated Lia even more than Maguire for eating all that food.

I looked at the farm animals in their pens and felt a sense of envy. At least they were fed and looked after. But that made me feel even more embittered. I grabbed a pitchfork leaning against a wall and started waving it around. Then I heard the pigs squealing. I was shaking and tears were running down my face. I stepped into the pen and started stabbing at the pigs.

As I got more and more angry, I thrust the pitchfork deeper and deeper into them. They were screaming with fear and pain. The noise was so unbearable that I decided to put them completely out of their agony. I ended up killing eight of them stone dead without feeling any guilt. The pigs were just the first thing I'd come across. God knows what I would have done if I'd encountered a human being when I was in that mood.

The woman who owned the pigs had seen me slaughter them and, within minutes of getting back home, there was a delegation knocking at the door demanding retribution for what I'd done. The woman who owned the animals said I ought to be put away for killing them. They were baying for my blood.

The strange thing was that Maguire seemed to understand the reasons why I'd lost my marbles like that. He even whispered to me that day, 'I'm going to start beating you up in the street where everyone can see it. Every time I hit you, you scream out and shout but I won't be hitting you that hard.'

So he kicked me from where those dead pigs were still lying in the mud all the way back to the room. Everyone heard it.

Maguire controlled me totally. In the end, everyone knew we were thieves and we even used to tease the shopkeepers by walking past their shops and singing,

'Here's the robbers passing by, passing by, passing by.'

As I've said, he was a real-life Fagin, and I continued to do his dirty work. Under orders from Maguire, I stole a tea-chest off the back of a lorry, hid it away and then nicked some scales and brown paper bags from a local shop and went knocking on people's doors, selling the tea from a stolen blue pram. Eventually, we knocked on a nun's door and she grassed us up and we all got nicked.

And still Mrs Mulchrone kept coming back to haunt me.

One time, I went to confession in a local church and told the priest all about Mrs Mulchrone. He said she didn't matter because it was a long time ago. I said I had to talk about her.

Then this priest said, 'Are you telling me everything, my son?'

'What?' I replied.

'Do you have dirty thoughts?'

It was then I realised he was masturbating. I got up and slammed the door to the confessional box shut and never went to confession ever again.

It wasn't until many years later that I decided to see a psychiatrist in Harley Street about Mrs Mulchrone. But after just 15 minutes this quack said to me, 'You better leave.'

I said, 'Why?'

He then said, 'I can't help you.'

The psychiatrist said my life as a child had been so bad there was no point in trying to turn the clock back. It seemed appalling that a so-called expert could just turn his back on me but afterwards I realised what he meant. There was nothing he could do which would change the past for me. I had to learn to deal with it myself.

I still believe that stealing that money from Mrs Mulchrone was the worst thing I've done in my life. But I never use it as an excuse for what happened to me in later life. Mrs Mulchrone just represents the guilt I feel.

I ended up going to live in London where I eventually became a property developer after an early life living on the edge of the criminal underworld. Today I'm a big benefactor to many charities and half the reason is because I feel I've got to give something back. Mrs Mulchrone remains a huge presence in my life and I still feel I haven't fully paid the price for what I did to her.

But at least I've now got a happy, settled family and we all live in a big house in an expensive area and I am a successful businessman. I just wish I could do something to alleviate the pain and guilt but I guess it will be with me for the rest of my life.

3

Janey

MY MUM DEEVA was a very beautiful, exotic-looking Indian woman in her prime when I was born. Men used to admire her and she positively lapped up all their attention. I suppose it made her feel like someone important. On the council estate where I was brought up, there weren't many single Asian mothers and my mum, in her tight-fitting black pencil skirts and high heels, certainly turned a few heads.

We lived in Hounslow, in west London, in a grim-looking, grey four-storey building constructed in the 1960s. It looked and felt like a prison to me when I was a young girl. There was no carpet in our flat and it really lacked the creature comforts. The constant noise of planes flying overhead on their way to nearby Heathrow Airport added to the odd, impersonal atmosphere. One moment complete silence, the next a jumbo thundering overhead. It was enough to do anyone's head in.

The first 'bad thing' I can remember was when my mum tried to make me suck her breasts. I was about four at the time. It definitely wasn't about her trying to feed me like a baby because she also took my hand and tried to push it up her skirt. It didn't mean much to me back then because I was so young. It was only when I later started to get flashbacks about what had happened that I realised what she'd done was all wrong.

Back then, Mum would leave me in the house on my own while she went off for the night. She'd often go up to Earls Court when she was on the game. She'd lock me in that flat, even though I wasn't five years old at the time. She never got anyone to look after me and then in the early hours she'd come rolling back smelling of cheap perfume and booze.

Sometimes, she'd walk into my bedroom, start shaking me and then pull me out of the bed.

'Come on, Janey. Come with me. I've got someone I want you to meet.'

Then I'd be made to make a bed on the floor of her bedroom with some blankets while she had sex with a stranger. There was never any explanation from her. Not a word. None of the men seemed bothered that a kid was in the room being made to watch them. They seemed to think it was all just a laugh. I don't remember one of them ever objecting or telling my mum to get me out of the room.

The blokes came from everywhere: punters from the West End, geezers from the pub, others from the estate where we lived. You name it. My mum even had sex with cabbies if she couldn't afford the fare home. Even now, I could go down to certain pubs and there'd be blokes there who've slept with my mum. A lot of them adored her. She was a beautiful, exotic creature who looked and acted differently from other people.

Mum had one regular called Patrick, a funny-looking little Irish man, and he seemed all right just because he was a familiar face, unlike most of them. I don't know if he paid my mum for it or not but I used to bump into him going in and out of a pub near our home. Often, it seemed like every bloke in Hounslow had had it off with my mum.

I walked into a local pub only a few months back and there was yet another bloke who'd slept with her. His name was Robbie. When I was a kid, he'd once told me, 'I'm going to get you in bed and I'm gonna do you.' I even remember my mum trying to get me to go and sit on Robbie's lap and stuff like that.

Robbie was about 40 back then. He was horrible. When I saw him in the pub recently, I turned round and walked right back out of there. I was shaking like a leaf.

Back in the early days, I didn't even realise who these men were – that they'd mostly paid to sleep with my mum. I remember there was this Indian man called Hari and one day I walked in the front room of our flat and there he was, sitting on the sofa watching telly. Hari made me sit on his lap. I used to suck my thumb back then. I was about six at the time and it was a bit of a nervous reaction. Anyway, I remember him trying to pull my thumb out so he could stick his thing in my mouth. I ran off when he tried it on and thank God he never came after me. My mum wasn't even in the flat at the time. She was out somewhere. Probably on the game but I can't actually remember.

This bloke Hari was one of my mum's so-called special Indian friends and he was a local cricketer from nearby Ealing. After I told my aunt what had happened, she made sure I never saw him again. I was always asking my mum who these strange men were but she'd never answer except to say, 'Fuck off and mind yer own business.'

I always had good clothes because Mum shoplifted them all and she was good at it. Trouble was, she'd often disappear for a couple of days on her 'shopping trips' and leave me alone in the flat. I used to get so worried about her when she was gone. She never left me any proper food and I lived on cereal or whatever was there.

In many ways, I became the mother and she was the child. Sometimes she'd come home with two blacks eyes, cuts and bruises and I'd demand to know what had happened to her. She'd say she'd had a fight but wouldn't say with whom. One of the main hostess clubs in the West End where she worked was owned by a family who lived near us in Hounslow. They had a council house but it had posh white leather sofas and stuff like that so we all looked up to these people as being rich. I was always happier if Mum worked in their club because at least it was safer than being on the streets.

Virtually every night I lay in bed awake with this threat hanging over me that Mum would bring a bad man back with her. I never slept well anyway because my mum would say the 'bogeymen' were after me to stop me trying to leave the house while she was out. She'd always go on about them as she locked me in. She also said that if I ever left the house I would get the beating of a lifetime. So, from the age of four or five, I used to secretly slip next door. Once I'd heard my mum lock the door and go off in a cab then I'd bang on the wall to the neighbour who'd come round to the front window. She'd push it as I clicked the safety catch and out I'd get. Then they'd put me back in at about four or five in the morning before Mum got home.

One time Mum came back early and I got in big trouble. She screamed abuse at the neighbour and gave me a right beating. They never called the police because you just didn't do that where I came from. But those neighbours really cared about me. They were good people. They had a boy my age and a daughter. They were both 'teddies' and the dad had greased back hair and wore thick crepe-soled shoes which, ironically, were known as brothel creepers. I remember whenever I got put back in my mum's flat, the wife would bang on the wall to make sure I was back safely in my bedroom.

She'd also feed me in her house. The husband always gave me cuddles and I remember I often used to say to them, 'Will you be my mum and dad because my mum's not very nice to me?' But, despite all the problems, there was this natural instinct not to grass up my mum to the police. The neighbours said to me many years later that they couldn't do that to me because I still loved my mum so much and they could see that. You see, my mum was my only real connection with the world.

Without her, I had nothing. There was no other world out there for me.

Those nights when my mum was out working as a prostitute often went like this: the key would go in the door, there'd be a noise as she stumbled in the flat with a man. Then they'd go downstairs to the front room for a drink and the record player would go on. One of her favourites was 'Rock the Boat' – 'Don't rock the boat, baby...'

She also loved 'Sympathy for the Devil' by the Rolling Stones. We had loads of albums because a friend of my mum's gave them to us and Mum would play them on a cheap stereo record player. It had a smoky glass door with a crack through it and the needle jumped every few seconds. My mum loved music because she'd also done go-go dancing as well as escort work at hostess clubs when she wasn't on the streets.

Then after a few drinks Mum would come into my bedroom and make me follow her downstairs into the front room where I'd have to sit and watch them. 'Come on, Janey. Play the game,' was about all she ever said.

When I turned nine, the social services took me in. My mum then pushed me in and out of care whenever it suited her. Eventually, the council got a court order and tried to take complete control of my life. Easier said than done. I'd go to a children's home only to come back to Mum's at regular intervals. You see, I never actually told them the full story about what had happened to me. They knew my mum was on the game but they had no idea what she was doing to me. I kept it all bottled up because, despite everything, I felt the need to protect her. I don't know why. I've asked myself this question so many times but all I can conclude is that despite the abuse I still felt attached to my mum. It was as if it was her and me against the world.

Yet back in my bed at Mum's flat, I'd shut my eyes tightly and try to pretend to be asleep whenever I heard that key in the lock. I'd curl up in a tightly wound ball under the quilt. I remember another time my mum dragged me down to the lounge yet again to meet one of her blokes. One moment they were laughing and joking and then suddenly this man went mad. They were fighting each other like cat and dog. I remember the man then pulled a knife out and put it to my mum's neck. He dug it in so deep that a droplet of blood dribbled down between her breasts. Then I started screaming and screaming.

'STOP IT! PLEASE STOP IT!'

But they were so wrapped up in fighting and booze they didn't even notice me. I ran out of the house and knocked on the neighbours' door once again. My mum didn't even bother chasing after me and when I slipped quietly back into the house a few hours later that evil bastard who'd tried to kill my mum had gone and she was passed out drunk on the settee.

Then there was the time my mum had the hump with me after my dad had said he was coming to see us and he hadn't turned up. I was sitting on the sofa watching TV when she went to the kitchen and got out a bread knife. She was standing across me and lent down and ran the serrated edge of the knife under my toes, which cut and started bleeding. I screamed. I've got a scar on one toe to prove it to this day. Then she just walked off back into the kitchen and slung the knife in the drawer. I hopped up the stairs crying and got some toilet paper and wrapped it around my foot. About two days later I showed it to my grandmum and she flipped out at my mum. But my mum never said a word about it again. It was yet another unmentionable subject.

Not long afterwards. Mum turned up at a friend's house in Hammersmith because I'd run away and refused to go home to her. I remember feeling surprised that she even cared. I shouted abuse at her as we left that friend's house and we had a vicious fight in the street. She bit me just above my right eye and I still have the scar to prove it. The strange thing is, that scar will always remind me of a time when she actually showed that she cared.

I remember at one stage I made myself a little home in a cupboard under the stairs. I called it my escape hatch. I cleared all this rubbish out and made it into a small den all of my own. I'd lock myself in this cupboard and make phone calls on a pretend phone. I'd play little games with myself, like I was a receptionist running a switchboard. My imagination became a means of escape from the depraved world my mother had created.

She'd know I was in the cupboard but leave me alone until the drink really kicked in and then she'd start banging on the door trying to make me into her servant. 'Get this, get that.' She'd be getting drunker and drunker. Once she was with this punter and tried to get me to serve them booze in bed. I said, 'No, Mum, I'm not doing it.' I got a right slapping in front of this bloke for daring to stand up to her. He never said a word as far as I remember.

Sometimes I had a right go at the men in the house and called them perverts but none of them seemed too bothered. They just laughed at me. And many of them still kept trying to grab my hand and say, 'Come on, come and sit on my knee.' I'd go 'Fuck off.'

I've watched that Indian film *Bride and Prejudice* tons of times since it came out and I cry every time, because that's what my mum's family were like. They tried so hard to force me into an arranged marriage. They introduced me to this Indian boy when I was nine. He lived in Ealing and I was in a home at the time but my grandfather arranged it so this boy's family didn't even know I was in any trouble. I remember this boy telling me how his parents had arranged for us to marry. He was 12 or 13 at the time. The family were loaded but then I went and ruined it all by swearing at him. My grandfather never forgave me.

But then my grandfather was a truly evil character. My mum was always saying how she'd get him one day. She'd say, 'He's a very bad man, a fuckin' bastard and one day I kill him.' My mum even decided she'd been adopted to make herself feel better. My grandfather certainly did give her a few black eyes over the years but she gave as good as she got. Takes one to know one, I guess. Even my aunt beat me sometimes. As a result, I was very aggressive and I wouldn't take any shit off anyone.

I sometimes wished there'd be a knock on our front door and the nightmare of my life with Mum would be completely exposed – but it never happened. Around the time when Mum was trying to get me to actually go to bed with her punters, I got friendly with this woman on the estate called Sue.

She became like my mentor and one day she had a screaming match with my mum, who'd always denied what was happening. Afterwards, I got a severe beating from mum.

'Stop making up these lies, Janey,' she yelled at me in that strong Indian accent. 'You fuckin' little bastard.'

Funny thing is that she was right – I was a bastard because she'd never married my dad.

If I answered Mum back or swore at her, she'd straighten out metal coat hangers and then fold them in half and beat me everywhere with them. On my back, on my arms and legs, even sometimes on my face. I'd often be running up the stairs to try and get away from her. Once, just after yet another punter had left the house, she started with the coat hanger and screamed wildly at me, 'Your dad's not your dad. The real one lives abroad. You've got plenty of brothers and sisters as well.'

I completely lost it after that and smashed up the entire flat. Then I locked myself in the bathroom with a screwdriver, which I pointed away from the door and towards my head. I remember Mum banging on the door and I shouted at her, 'If you kick the door down the screwdriver's gonna go through my head.'

Eventually, she stopped and calmed down but I wouldn't come out of the bathroom and stayed there sobbing for at least four hours. Finally, I emerged and went downstairs and lay on the sofa and started screaming over and over again, 'I want my dad. I want my dad. I want my dad.' I kept repeating it. Then my mum rang my dad. He said he'd come but he never appeared. That was typical.

Dad was always saying he'd come and then never turn up. He was nicer to me when I actually got to see him, but really he wasn't that interested in getting lumbered with me, which is probably why he failed to show up so often. I was so desperate for Dad's love and approval that I more or less forgave him everything, because the one thing he never did was treat me like Mum did and I was grateful for that. His home should have been a place of refuge for me but it just never turned out that way.

My mum and dad had originally split up when I was three. There were many times when I would phone up my dad and tell him that Mum was trying to get me to do things with strange men but he never did anything about it. I don't think he believed me.

Mum used me to get at my dad because it was only after he met his next girlfriend that they stopped sleeping together. She just wanted to hurt my dad. She'd say to him, 'Janey's not my daughter no more. You gotta come and get her.' She was always trying to drive a wedge between us. She made me think she didn't give a shit about me.

The story of my childhood was that no one ever wanted to get involved. I was even shipped out to India to stay with an aunt at one stage, but I never told her what was happening at home. My mum got rid of me when she'd had enough of me whether it was to a children's home or to a relative.

Throughout all this time, she took vast amounts of Valium sleeping tablets. She'd get dozens at a time from her doctor. So she rarely got up before lunchtime. The flat was disgustingly dirty. The neighbours would spot me frantically cleaning the flat some mornings and even helped me polish the bits I couldn't reach. I also used to always wash my own clothes in the bath.

When Mum was off her head on Valium, she would just lie on the sofa, chain-smoking and watching telly. School was a long walk away, but she didn't care about whether I went or not. Occasionally, she'd go up the shops but more often she'd spend whatever she'd earned after a night on the game in the bookies. She loved the horses. I'd come out of school at lunch sometimes and see her or hear her screaming from inside the bookies. 'Go on, my son!' she'd yell at the horses. If she'd had a lucky day I'd even get a decent take-out dinner that night.

Mum tried to cook sometimes but she wasn't much good at it and most of the stuff in the kitchen was rotten and filthy. As I got older, I used to cook myself bread curry with curry powder, tomato and onions a lot of the time.

But, in the middle of all this, my mum got even more reckless. I'd get home from school and she'd be in the front room having it off with some bloke. Other times her 'rumping' happened in her bedroom next to mine and you could hear everything because the walls were so thin.

The neighbour who lived next door and regularly rescued me later told me she could hear me screaming when my mum beat me. Mum would order me not to ever talk to the neighbour and she'd always slam the door in her face if the neighbour came round to complain. Mum said I was making up lies. That was the only way my mum could deal with what happened between us.

My first proper children's home was in Surrey. This was quickly followed by one in Twickenham. Then came another one in Acton, then a place called Hampshire Lodge, before I ended up in Cornwall. Every time I absconded, they sent me further away from my home. The funny thing is that I ran away from those homes because I didn't like the way I felt locked up. I'd scarper and turn up at a friend's house in London, then I'd get desperate and go home to Mum. I still had this weird sense of responsibility for

Mum which made me pop home to see if she was OK, despite all the bad things she had caused.

In one children's home, I encountered another form of abuse – but at least it was only physical. If you didn't do what the staff wanted, they gave you a kick up the arse or a punch in the back of the head. If you back-chatted them, they'd go mental and, if you lost your temper, they'd throw you in this room next to the TV room. Everyone would be told to leave the area if a beating was in the air. Then a load of staff members would come in and teach you a lesson. They used to call me all sorts of horrible names. I would try and fight back but it was usually three big men thrashing me and punching me. I'd be left there a few hours until I'd calmed down.

My mum came to visit me in Cornwall once but she was so pissed they sent her straight home. Another time I was in a home in west London and she brought this regular boyfriend who seemed all right because he gave me some gold earrings. I wasn't used to people being nice to me unless they wanted something in exchange.

My mum brought me fags from the age of nine. She'd slip them to me under the table during visiting time. She even pushed a bit of money into my hand if she had any. The funny thing with my mum was that there were loving times with her, despite all the abuse. I'm sure part of her did love me but the other side of her must have hated me so much. Sometimes my mum even cuddled me on the sofa at her home and was loving towards me but she never talked about what had happened between us. But then I never questioned what she'd done to me. We'd have screaming matches about petty little things but nothing serious. She never justified what she did to me. She just acted as if it had never happened.

Yet I remained to the outside world a well-dressed kid thanks to Mum's shoplifting. Her favourite store was Marks and Spencer. And when I was home I turned my bedroom into a cosy little shrine away from all the madness by putting posters on every inch of wall space. I also had this thick patchwork quilt filled with duckfeathers. It had been made for me by an elderly aunt of my dad's, who turned up once a week with delicious home-baked cakes and sometimes helped me clean the flat. I never told her what was happening to me at home either, because of that same twisted sense of loyalty towards Mum. Something inside me stopped me from grassing her up. I just couldn't do it.

On the estate where we lived, many of the single mums had what they called house parties in their flats. Local men used to turn up like bees to a honeypot. Many of these parties were held in Mum's maisonette. The older I got, the more my mum tried to involve me with her and her boyfriends, especially when she was hosting those parties. She'd say to me, 'Why don't you come to bed with us?' She'd be lying there with yet another bloke, trying to encourage me and then I'd run out in tears. And she never bothered chasing me because she knew I wouldn't grass her up. I did tell the neighbours next door a few details, but never the *complete* story. That lady neighbour later told me that as I got older I became more intense and I did actually describe some of what my mum was trying to get me to do. There was mention of a vibrator at one stage. I can't even bear to think what she tried to do to me with it.

As I got older I became much more aggressive and told all my mum's blokes where to go. One time, I phoned up this tough character who knew my dad and asked him for help. He came round and beat up a couple of men who were trying it on with me. I have to admit I enjoyed watching them having their faces mashed in.

The only time the police came knocking on my mum's door was when I ran away from children's homes. They called it 'dawn banging' and they'd show up at five in the morning and break the door down. They'd be with social workers and my mum would tell them all to fuck off and she was very aggressive.

She'd threaten them with anything, knives, you name it and she'd say she was going to kill them all. One social worker got so scared she ran out of the flat and came back later with reinforcements.

When I was in my early teens, I started going through a punk stage and one day I was waiting round at my mum's friend's flat to pick up a pair of boots. My mum was running around this flat in a pair of knickers and just a fox fur flying around her neck and these other two women were having sex with this friend of the family right in front of me. In the middle of all this, my mum and this other woman gave me a load of Polaroid photos in a bag and told me to take them around to my dad's house. I suppose they were trying to wind him up. I secretly looked inside the bag after leaving the flat and saw snaps of them all having sex. But I was already well past the point of being shocked by anything any more. I just put them back in the bag and went to my father's house as instructed.

When I got there, one of his friends slapped me around the face because he thought I was involved in it all. It seemed like there was always someone there to punish and hurt me. I couldn't win. My dad's friend later apologised to me. I also heard a story that this same man was my real dad, which was rubbish but it hurt.

Then my mum started on about how my real dad was living in Spain. I reckon that was because she'd lived and worked there as a go-go dancer. She even spoke fluent Spanish. But she never explained any more. I just prayed that she was lying.

My alleged dad was the opposite in many ways. He never once hit me and, when I was younger, I'd had a lot to do with him. We were very close but, when this other woman had children by my dad, I wasn't wanted on the scene any more. Once or twice Mum went round to their house and attacked this woman and demanded to know why she was having a relationship with Dad.

Another time I turned all my anger and frustration on my mum and ended up beating her up. It happened when I arranged a 'blues party' – which was just for black people on the estate – at my mum's flat. I'd charged them all three quid on the door. I must have been about 13 at the time.

Anyway, I just flipped out at Mum. I can't even remember what started it all. But there was a lot of anger inside me about everything she'd ever done to me down the years and all the situations she'd exposed me to. I started punching her very hard and eventually slammed her against a wall. Blood spurted everywhere and smeared down the wallpaper as she slid to the floor. Then I stormed out of the house.

Mum was raped by four black blokes at that blues party. These men attacked her with a bottle and she had to have about 45 stitches after a neighbour took her to hospital. No one was arrested for raping her because yet again she wouldn't involve the police. I knew who it was. I used to see them on the estate the whole time. Some of them are still there to this day.

I left my mum's house after that and went to yet another children's home. From then on, whenever I was on weekend leave, I never went near her and stayed with my friend Sue instead. She was a mum herself with two young kids and she provided me with a sense of security. The children's home in Cornwall actually paid Sue to look after me for the weekend instead of my mum, because she was deemed to be 'a responsible adult'. She'd get £27 and give me most of the money. I even bumped into my mum in the local pub but we didn't stop to chat. Strange way to handle your own parent, ain't it?

Sometimes I went to my dad's home in Hammersmith and one of our favourite hangouts was nearby Earls Court, where many vice girls worked the streets looking for business. I'd go up there with a few mates and pretend to be on the game and then nick punters' cash, credit cards, wallets and stuff like that. Then I started spotting my own mum walking the streets, leaning into men's cars or strolling arm-in-arm towards the nearby rundown hotels and hostels.

After a few visits to Earls Court, my mum started coming up and chatting with me. One time she told me she had a rich Arab punter who'd pay good money to take me abroad with him. I know I was 13 at the time because this man was willing to pay a grand for every year of my age and I remember she said he'd pay her thirteen grand. She said, 'Go on. It's good money and then you won't have to go back to that children's home no more.' I said no way.

Other times in Earls Court I'd bump into Mum after she'd pulled a punter and I'd go with her and sit outside the hotel while she did the business with them. Then we'd go off for a meal together. One time, this bloke in a red Ferrari pulled up with a big black suitcase in the back. They went off to this seedy hotel nearby. Forty-five minutes later, I'm still waiting outside the hotel and I'm getting really worried. Then suddenly Mum comes down the steps of the hotel looking really shocked and says nothing. I'm even more worried by then. Then we get to the end of the street and she starts laughing her head off because he'd made her put a bib on him and a nappy and all that sort of gear, and she thought it was hilarious. She even put a baby's bottle in his mouth to suck on. And all the time I'd been worrying she'd got herself hurt. I don't think my mum ever realised the stress she put me through.

My mum was also well known at posh hotels on Park Lane in the West End. She said she bunged some of the staff a few bob to let her in. One time Mum nicked a big brown bag off a punter, which turned out to be full of pure heroin. I remember she gave it to my dad and told him she didn't know what to do with it and that he should sell it. It must have been about two ounces of heroin. God knows what he did with it.

Out on the streets, Mum got beaten up regularly by punters. One time a car door was smashed in her face and her eye almost came out the socket. I'm convinced that attack sent her around the twist because afterwards she went even more mental.

Back at that children's home in Cornwall, I was kept in for absconding yet again. I even pretended I'd stabbed someone so it made me look harder than I really was. I dyed my hair orange. I'd done glue from the age of nine and now I was back on it with a vengeance. I'd also been nicking more and more of my mum's Valium and selling them. I was drinking, smoking and at 11 I'd even snorted cocaine for the first time. We also used to pop speed pills we got off doctors who prescribed them for slimming.

Looking back on it, none of the adults in my

family ever showed any real concern for me. One time when I'd just turned 13, I was dressed up by one of my dad's girlfriends and taken to the pub. I got really drunk and ended up back in this woman's flat. Next to me on the bed she was having sex with this man she'd met in the pub. I turned over and cried silently into my pillow.

Just after this I was once again on the run from a children's home and went back to my mum's flat for a few days. My mum introduced me to this boy of 16 or 17 who ended up being my first boyfriend. I thought it was love at first sight.

On our first night together, I was out of my head on Valium, which Mum had encouraged me to take, and she locked me in my bedroom at her flat with this bloke and he took my virginity. I was just 13. I remember drifting in and out of consciousness as he did what he wanted to me. I woke up in the morning and only realised I'd lost my virginity because there was blood on the sheets. That morning over breakfast she made a joke of what had happened and said to me, 'Oh, I fucked him last week. He's all right.' She asked me if I'd enjoyed it. I didn't reply. I closed my mind to her cruel words. I was devastated but so desperate for the relationship to work that I didn't confront the boy about sleeping with my mum.

That first so-called boyfriend was so brutal. He'd

70

proudly tell me how he was going to take me and hurt me each time. I let him do it to me because I was so out of it on Valium and other drugs. I'd say I didn't want to do it and he'd just ignore me. I remember crying one time and he held me by the throat and said I had to let him do it. Sometimes he even invited his mates in to watch us 'perform'. I'd already been put off sex by my mum's behaviour; now I positively hated it.

I floated around for about a year on the run at this time. I was taking at least two Valium a day. I was like a walking zombie. I was so spaced out I didn't want to face reality. I even also went back to glue-sniffing yet again.

When I was 14, my dad's mum wanted to adopt me and for me to go and live with her in Ireland. But Mum wouldn't allow it and neither Dad nor his relatives had the courage to take her on. Everybody knew what was going on with Mum but no one did anything to stop it. If I so much as spilled a drink or if Mum's flat wasn't tidy, she'd go crazy. She'd pull me by the hair and then slap me. Once I tried to slide under the bed to hide from her but it was too low and I got stuck halfway. She got out the coat hanger and made me suffer.

She'd often scream at me and say it was my fault that she'd split up with my dad. Everything was always my fault. According to her, I'd caused all the problems in the world. Eventually, I started to believe she must be right. Maybe it would be better if I wasn't alive to cause all this trouble.

So I tried to kill myself by swallowing dozens of my mum's Valium tablets. I remember my mum and a friend walked me around the estate slapping my face to keep me awake. Then Mum stuck her fingers down my throat. But she never called an ambulance because she didn't want the police involved. Luckily I recovered.

Looking back on it now, I realise Mum never dealt with what happened in her own life. It was only a few years ago I decided to try and get to the bottom of all this. When I was at that children's home in Cornwall, I used to wander around thinking I'd imagined it all. I couldn't work out if it had really happened or not.

I was so confused. I actually convinced myself that maybe I was just coming out with this stuff in sympathy with the other kids in the home, who'd also suffered serious parental abuse. Maybe I just wanted them to feel sorry for me.

The first time I completely opened up about it was to my dad's second wife when I was about 15 or 16. But then she made out I'd said it was my dad who'd abused me which simply wasn't true. Up to then, I had never told anyone and now I was regretting ever opening my big trap. I'd always assumed that everyone else's life was as bad if not worse than mine. We lived on such a rough estate that maybe I felt all this was normal.

This all sent me completely off my rocker. Then I sat down and discussed it with my then boyfriend's mother in Cornwall. She was the only person who understood what I'd been through because a similar thing had happened to her. I asked her if she thought I was going mad. She assured me I was not and gave me the confidence to try and deal with what had happened.

I even went back to Mum's estate in Hounslow and traced my next-door neighbour because I had to know if it really had all happened. That neighbour confirmed everything. But knowing that didn't make me hate my mum. It just solved the mystery of where all those evil, appalling images had come from in the first place. Then I confronted Mum and, as usual, she denied it completely. I was back to square one. How could she pretend it never happened?

Not long after this I met a boy called Mickey and got pregnant. I was 17 years old but delighted to have something to look forward to. My baby son Thomas became the most important thing in my life. Social services provided me with a nice little flat in west

London near where my dad lived. I split with the father of my child but he proved himself a good dad by visiting little Thomas regularly. Being away from Mum helped improve my relationship with her, despite everything that had happened.

But happiness never lasts long when my mum is around. My mum started visiting me once a month, and one day she had Thomas on her knee. I didn't like leaving her in a room with him on her own, so I was always around if she was near my child. As I watched her, she smiled at me strangely and then asked me when I'd let him have sex. She said it as calmly as if she was asking about my holiday plans. I completely flipped and ordered her out of the house.

I remember looking at the blank expression on her face that day and I'd swear she just didn't understand she'd said something wrong. After that, I confronted her every time we met and she kept saying it was all lies and that I was making everything up.

By this time, Mum was in her forties and had put on a lot of weight and was living on benefit in a block of flats for people with mental-health problems. They even had their own matron and everything. My mum stank and one of her front teeth was missing. But she still had that pretty face and remained convinced she was a sex symbol. And she continued to be mad about my dad.

But she never once dealt with my issues. Sometimes she told me she hated me and I was the ugliest person in the world. Other times she said I was beautiful. But she made it crystal clear on many occasions that she didn't want me. She only wanted my dad. She'd wait for him until the day she died. One time, she even asked me to get a jar of my dad's sperm so she could get herself pregnant by him.

I was even more embarrassed by my mum when she got older. A friend of mine called Peter was shocked when she started talking dirty in front of him. She had these mad eyes and would say she worked for the FBI and 'I scalp people'. I reckon it was the guilt about her past that sent her over the edge.

But she never once talked about her childhood. I phoned up one of my aunts and told her about all the abuse and she told me she'd always known about it. They all knew. My granddad, mum's father, tried to snog me once and I know he went to prostitutes and peep shows. I'm also convinced my mum slept with her dad. My granddad had four daughters and he moved a lot because in those days as an Indian you had to get your daughters married off so you kept moving until you found suitable husbands.

Maybe it's a tragedy that Mum never actually married anyone. She had many abortions. She used sex as the ultimate currency – with probation officers, doctors or anyone who could help her. She'd tell me all about it. We'd turn up at her probation officer and she'd plonk me outside and say, 'I'm going to do him so you wait here.' She'd be due to go to court and the case would suddenly get dropped. She used sex as the ultimate form of manipulation. I never dared tell anyone like that probation officer what had happened during my childhood. How could I trust someone who was having sex with my mum?

I've tried my hardest to come to terms with what my mum did to me. The scars she's left on me will never properly heal, partly because she never accepted responsibility for what happened and never said sorry.

Now I'm in a steady relationship with two beautiful kids and I'm so determined never to repeat history. I keep a spotlessly clean home and I try to encourage my kids to remain children for as long as possible. I don't want to expose them to anything that might ruin their childhood in the way mine was taken away from me at such an early age.

I suppose in many ways I'm lucky because somehow I survived my childhood and have come out the other side with a life and a family I can be truly proud of. But why did it all have to happen in the first place? I still wish I had the answer but, when my mother died a few years ago from a heart attack at the relatively young age of 50, I knew then that I'd never know why. I hope she's in a better place now than when she was on this earth. Her troubled life affected so many people. Yet ultimately she was the biggest victim of all.

4

John

I WAS BORN in Southampton in 1945. My full name is John Derek Katuin. My father's name was Aire, which is Dutch for Harry, and my mother was Joyce Ruby and my grandmother (her mother) was called Vera Maynard. My dad was a Dutch seaman, but I never met him because he refused to move to Southampton to live with my mum after they got married during the war. My first memory is of my mum sitting me outside the pub where she worked in a pram with a Britvic bottle and a teat while she did the dishes inside.

When I was little, a quietly spoken Scotsman called Alex Jamieson came on the scene. He was a big mountain of a man from the Gorbals of Glasgow and worked in the construction industry. Mum was 23 and Alex about 28 when they first met. I'll never forget the first day he turned up at our house and Mum introduced him to me and my older brother Terry as our new dad. That was it. No real explanation, just a simple announcement. Now we had a new father. Alex didn't say much but I remember thinking he was a scary-looking character because he seemed so big.

Not long after that, we all moved to the Hampshire village of Blackfield, about 30 miles from Southampton. I must have been about three or four years old and I was so excited to be living in the countryside. Blackfield seemed like a million miles away from the bombsites of Southampton. This was to be a fantastic time for us all as a family. My new dad Alex didn't seem so scary after all. In any case, we hardly saw him because he was out at work most of the time. Me and my brother Terry, who was a year older than me, led an idyllic life running through rolling fields, attending a local school with just a few classmates and getting up to mischief in the nearby streams and valleys.

Mum seemed very happy in Blackfield. The school was so small that we both got special attention from the teachers. I was a well-adjusted kid back then and never had a fight with anyone the whole time we lived in Blackfield. It just wasn't that sort of place. My abiding memory of those days in the countryside was of me and Terry running through these massive cornfields, hiding up trees and playing hide and seek. We'd often spend entire days exploring the countryside and no one ever worried about where we were because it was safe back then. We had a load of friends in the village and Mum seemed so happy not to be in the big city.

Alex even seemed a decent sort of bloke. He used to drive Mum and us to places like Stonehenge for the day where we'd have a picnic. Even when Terry and I mucked about in the back of the car, he took it all in good spirits. I often remember looking across at Mum and seeing a broad smile on her face as she watched us in the back of Alex's car. She'd had a tough old time before he'd come on the scene, but now we were all one secure family unit and it couldn't get much better than that.

Most weeks, Alex was away working so our lives really centred around our mum. And, looking back on it now, I suppose he did keep himself to himself when he was at home and didn't have that much to do with us kids. Mum adored Alex and always made sure there was a meal waiting for him when he got home. We'd often eaten by then and would be playing in our bedroom or out in the fields so we didn't see him most evenings either.

But, about five years after moving to Blackfield, Alex lost his job and things changed virtually overnight. We had to leave the countryside and move back to grimy, grey Southampton. Terry and I were heartbroken because we'd loved it in the village and I remember we kept asking Mum why we had to leave. She was too upset to give us a proper answer, but with Alex glaring in the car next to her I suppose I now realise why.

Initially, we moved into my nan's house in Graham Road, Southampton. It was very crowded and I soon realised Nan wasn't keen on Alex. There were furious rows late at night, which often woke up me and Terry. Sometimes cutlery was thrown and there was a lot of thumping but eventually things went quiet and the next morning there was never any mention of what had happened.

Within a few months, we'd moved out of Nan's into the top two floors of a big house at 34 Belvue Road, 600 yards from her house. Everything started to change after we got into that flat.

The first incident I remember was when I got home from school one afternoon and sat down at the kitchen table to read the *Southampton Evening Echo* newspaper. I recall rustling the paper as I changed pages. Just then, a voice bellowed at me from the other side of the room. 'Stop makin' that fuckin' noise, boy.' It was Alex. I'd never heard him speak so loudly before. Usually, you could hardly hear what he was saying. I looked up at him and nodded before going back to the newspaper. A few moments later, I turned the page once again. A strange, eerie silence filled the room then BANG! A hand flew across the back of my head. 'I said stop makin' that fuckin' noise, boy!' I put the newspaper down and went up to my bedroom without uttering another word.

That evening, I was banished from sitting with the rest of the family at supper. They all ate at the kitchen table while Mum told me I had to go in the next room and eat alone. I felt so miserable and unloved when I heard them all talking and laughing. From that day onwards, I was never allowed to sit with them all during mealtimes. Alex clearly hated me with such a passion that it made me feel like a nobody. The hatred oozed out of him whenever he so much as looked at me. I was soon getting a bashing from Alex at least four times a week. My once happy childhood had turned into a nightmare.

One day, I came home from school unusually early because sports had been cancelled and found the front door smashed in and hanging off its hinges. As I stepped into the hallway, I heard an ear-piercing scream that sounded like Mum. I rushed in to the kitchen to find Alex throttling her on the floor.

'STOP IT! STOP IT!' I yelled.

But he continued trying to squeeze the life out of Mum so I got on his back and grabbed him around the neck to pull him off her. But he was too strong for me and pushed me away with his arm. I fell back on to the floor before scrambling to the kitchen cabinet where I pulled a knife out of the drawer.

'STOP IT! PLEASE!' I pleaded, as I heard Mum struggling for breath.

I lunged at Alex with the knife but missed on three attempts. Then he let go of Mum and grabbed the knife from me and threw it on the floor. At least Mum was free. She lay there in an exhausted heap, wheezing for breath with his blotchy red fingermarks indented in her neck.

'YOU LITTLE BASTARD!' he yelled at me.

Then he grabbed me and began pummelling me into the floor. I curled up in a ball to try to avoid being seriously injured but the punches kept raining down on me.

'LET HIM GO, ALEX! PLEASE!' Mum shouted but the punches just kept coming.

Mum tried everything to get Alex to let me go of me but her fists on his back did little to stop him. She eventually managed to pull me away with him still trying to reach me with a flurry of long-arm punches as she pushed me up the stairs towards my bedroom.

She said she was going to lock me in for the rest of the day for my own protection.

I threw myself on the bed, crying tears more of frustration than pain because I felt I had failed to protect my mum properly. For a few seconds, there was silence in the flat then I heard Alex bellowing at Mum and this was followed by the unmistakable sounds of him once again attacking her.

I was soon shaking with anger and trying to open my door but it was impossible without a key. So I pulled up the bedroom window and looked down at the pavement three storeys below, took a deep breath and stepped out on to the drainpipe, which I shinned down at high speed. All the time I could hear Mum shouting, 'NO MORE, PLEASE, ALEX! NO MORE!'

I finally reached the pavement and got the old woman who lived underneath us to let me in the front door. I rushed back into the flat to confront Alex once again. This time he took one look at me and let go of Mum before storming out of the house and down to the pub where he no doubt drowned his sorrows. Mum and I collapsed in each other's arms in tears. That night, she locked me in my bedroom once again because she was so worried Alex might attack me again when he got back from the boozer.

The following morning ,I crept down the stairs, grabbed some breakfast and ran off to school before Alex even got up. It was a pattern that would continue for most of the rest of my childhood.

The atmosphere at home soon got so bad that I began doing extra school activities just to avoid being in that house of hate. Football practice, art classes, swimming, boxing, gymnastics – you name it. I was even invited to football trials at Southampton FC. I was vice-captain of the school football team. Anything to avoid coming home early and facing Alex. Why had it all come to this? I didn't know the answer because I was too young to work it out.

Not long afterwards, one of our neighbours, a Maltese man, was round at our home teaching me how to play guitar when Alex came rolling in pissed from the pub. He went ballistic when he saw this man and started pummelling him because he thought this neighbour was having an affair with Mum. Eventually, Alex dragged the man out into the street and knocked him to the pavement.

'Stay out of my house!' Alex yelled.

Meanwhile, Mum was pleading, 'He's only teaching John how to play guitar.'

Alex replied, 'I don't want a stranger in this house.'

After that, I used to sneak next door to get my guitar lessons.

Later that same day, Alex returned to the flat and started hitting me across the back of my head until I escaped up the stairs to my bedroom, which Mum once again locked behind me.

It got so bad I wasn't even allowed to talk in front of Alex. If I dared mutter a few words even to my own brother, he'd whack me across the back of the head. When we were watching cartoons on our black-and-white TV, he'd come in the room and switch the set off and then look defiantly at me for a reaction. Not a word of explanation, just that look of sheer hatred on his face. From then on, Mum would come rushing in and tell us if Alex was about to come in and that we should scarper.

Not surprisingly, I got in the habit of getting up and walking out of any room Alex was in to avoid a confrontation. But often he'd chase after me and slap me around the head and say, 'Where you going?'

'Upstairs.'

'You fuckin' stay there and sit down and shut yer mouth.'

Then he'd whack me again round the back of my head.

Mum would be in the kitchen cooking him a meal. I sometimes thought it was all a game to Alex. He'd lost his job and now he had a new occupation to keep himself amused – beating me. But, even when he eventually got some work as a plumber, it didn't stop him attacking me.

My brother Terry was terrified of Alex but never challenged him. As a result, Terry avoided beatings while I got hammered full on. But I refused to be intimidated by this bully of a man.

Alex rarely hit me in public. It was usually inside the house. That was his castle and he reckoned he could do whatever he liked in there. I think that must have been why I was made to eat in a different room. He never once explained to me what I had done wrong.

In fact, I can't remember him ever properly talking to me about anything. My life was turning into a war. I was about 11 or 12 by now and getting physically stronger, mainly thanks to all the school sporting activities I took part in to keep away from home. In school, I wouldn't tolerate anyone being bullied and I'd steam into the bullies so hard they never dared take me on. I suppose a lot of this was a reaction to what was happening to me at home.

Alex had sparked the violence within me and now I was trying to pay back all the bullies in the world. It was potentially a fatal combination and I was lucky never to come up against someone bigger and stronger than me at school.

Back at home, I started hitting Alex back whenever

he attacked me. I'd turn my body in a certain way to get maximum force out of hitting him. I hit those playground bullies the same way. But, for the moment, Alex remained much stronger than me and my retaliation against him provoked him to be even more brutal to me.

One time, I came home from school when I was about 12 and found a trail of blood in the hallway. Then I heard a plant pot smashing and I rushed into the sitting room to find Alex yet again on top of Mum with his hands at her throat.

'He's killing me, John. He's killing me!' she screeched.

I laid into him and pushed him on to the floor and started whacking him with a broom. He went mental and punched me straight in the face but somehow I kept on my feet and steamed into him again with the broom. He eventually grabbed the broom off me and started using it on me. 'I'll fuckin' kill ya!'

'Leave my mum alone! Leave my mum alone!'

Instead of throttling her, he then began smacking her across the head. She'd cut her arm and it was gushing out blood so I grabbed a blanket and tried to wrap it round her and help her away from him but he was still hitting out at her.

'Leave her alone! Leave her alone!'

Finally, he stopped and stormed out of the flat. I took Mum to hospital after the neighbours called an ambulance. I was distraught at the hospital that day when I took Mum in, but she begged me not to say anything to the police. 'Don't say nothing, John. Please don't say nothing.'

The police eventually came round to see her and asked her to press charges but she wouldn't. As usual, I never actually found out what that or any of the arguments were about. I started to think that Alex was simply addicted to violence.

The front door to the flat was smashed in at least two more times by Alex. He'd be drunk, forget his key and just break it down to get in. One time, I remember he stumbled in drunk and Mum said to him, 'Why don't you go off to bed?'

'Shut yer fuckin' mouth!' he yelled. 'Or I'll give ya a smackin'.' And he usually did just that.

Most nights, I'd rush straight upstairs if Alex was in. I even joined the Boys Brigade in order to stay out of the house even later. I was a life-boy as well. I also used to climb over the back wall at nights and help clean the leathers of a load of Australian speedway stars staying in the house next door. Anything to keep out of that house. I'd get back at about ten and creep quietly up the stairs while Alex was slumped in front of the telly.

The fear of going home was the worst part of my childhood. Hoping and praying that he wasn't there so I could avoid a beating. I genuinely feared that one day he might hurt me very badly, maybe even kill me.

His most fearful weapons were those enormous fists of his and he'd learned how to use them on the mean streets of Glasgow.

We all went up to Scotland one time to see his relatives and, of course, he was on his best behaviour then. He left me and Terry on his relatives' doorstep in the Gorbals while he went in with Mum. It was like he was ashamed of us. Then a gang of locals spotted us and started chucking stones at us. This was Alex's home turf and it reeked of violence.

Back home, my other granny hated Alex because she knew Mum and I were getting a beating from him all the time. Me and Mum would sometimes go together to my grandmother's house to get away from Alex when he was being violent.

Alex would drink whisky regularly at home and he would put the bottle down by the open fire so that the heat would made all the whisky on the side of the bottle go to the bottom so he could get an extra nip out of it. One time I picked up his precious bottle and asked Mum, 'What's this?'

She looked terrified. 'Put it back quickly before he sees you.'

Then Alex walked in and said, 'Who's been moving my whisky bottle about?' Then he looked straight at me. 'Is it you, John? It fuckin' is, ain't it?' Then he whacked me.

I'd often hear Alex knocking things over when he came in drunk. He'd sometimes stumble into our room to check I hadn't disappeared because I did that quite a lot. I could smell his doggy breath. Often I'd just go and sit in the garden or wander the streets. Then I'd come home really late when it was dark and climb up the drainpipe. It was much harder getting up than down.

When I was 12, Mum had a baby with Alex. His name was Andrew and, when I look back on it, the beatings got much worse after Andrew was born. I became even more of a 'non-person' in Alex's eyes. By this time, I was a distant child, uncommunicative, bitter, resentful and very untrusting. After Andrew was born, my brother Terry and I had to be even quieter in case we woke the baby.

One day, Alex came home while I was in the kitchen and I was trapped there because I couldn't get up the stairs to the bedroom without going past him and I didn't want another beating. Mum was out shopping. I started shivering with fear. Then he caught me glancing at him and said, 'What yer lookin' at?'

I didn't reply.

'I said, who're you lookin' at, yer little fucker?'

'Nobody. Leave me alone,' I muttered.

'Leave you alone! I'll fuckin' teach you!'

Then he charged into the kitchen and walloped me so hard I crashed to the floor. I remember looking up at him through blurred vision as he stood over me, arms crossed in defiance.

'I'm gonna teach you a lesson you'll never forget, sonny.'

I was too dazed to run. He got behind me and started throttling me with his hands. I could feel them digging into my neck. My windpipe closed tight. I could barely breathe. I tried to shout for help and started kicking anything close by in the hope the noise might raise the alarm before he killed me. Then Mum arrived at the front door and called out because she'd forgotten the key. No one answered. Then she heard a scuffle and knew that Alex was beating me so she smashed the glass of the door, let herself in and tried to rescue me.

Mum thumped Alex on the back to try to get him to release me. I was going purple in the face. I tried to elbow him in the stomach and then the face, but he ignored us both and continued throttling me with his bare hands. Then suddenly he let go of me, marched off towards the front door and headed off to the pub down the street.

Moments later, I stood in front of a mirror and saw

his fingerprints around my neck. The police turned up after being called by the neighbours. They saw my injuries and asked Mum to press charges against Alex. Then she pulled me aside and begged me not to tell the police what had happened. She'd only just had my half-brother Andrew at the time. 'Don't say nothin' to them, son. Please. Just say you were naughty or something.'

I was annoyed by her request at first. His fingerprints were still embedded in my neck and she wanted me to save his skin. But, back in those days, the mother had to officially make the charge because I was too young, so Mum made sure Alex got off yet again.

The beatings became like a never-ending cycle and I was getting more and more angry about being picked on by Alex. I went to hospital twice after he tried to strangle me. By the age of 14, I'd had enough of it. I was a reckless youth in every sense of the word and I was beginning not to care whether I lived or died.

Then me and a couple of mates broke into a local working men's club, got drunk and stole loads of booze. Looking back on it, I think I must have wanted to get nicked. Anything was better than living in that hell-hole with that animal Alex. Anyway, we brought some cases of whisky home and hid them in a bedroom cupboard.

Local TV news even reported that the club had been broken into. Later that same evening, the evil Alex smelled the booze on me and then, after I'd gone to sleep, tore the flat apart until he found the nicked whisky. He pulled me out of my bed, punched me so hard that he knocked me unconscious and then carried me over his shoulder across the local park and literally chucked me into the local police station. The coppers thought I'd been in an accident until Alex told them, 'This is the little bastard who nicked that booze.'

There was blood all over me and he told the coppers, 'He was trying to hit me so I bashed him up.' They just accepted it. I had blood smeared all over my face and two black eyes and they locked me in a cell. They didn't even call a doctor. Later, they pulled me into an interview room and said, 'Did you do it?'

I replied, 'Of course I did.'

That was it. All I wanted was to get away from Alex and that home of hate.

Some of the coppers felt sorry for me, but they said I'd still have to go away for breaking the law. I said I didn't give a fuck because I was just happy to escape from Alex. I had to get away, whatever the consequences. So I got sentenced to three years in an approved school.

My approved school was called Ashton Kings. The

headmaster was the brother of the writer James Joyce and he was a good man. I wasn't used to men being decent, fair-minded people, so it took a while for me to trust him. He was probably the first man I ever met who I liked. Up until then, men had represented nothing but hatred to me.

But sadly no one – including the headmaster – ever asked me what had happened to me at home. Back in those days, they didn't give much thought to domestic problems. I was a thief and I had to pay for my crimes. It was as simple as that.

Alex never came to see me in approved school, which was a relief, although naturally Mum visited regularly. She was very upset but I think that, in the back of her mind, she knew it was much easier for her with me out of the flat. I eventually forgot how bad things had been at home and started sorely missing Mum and my brother Terry. In the end, I ran away two or three times. But home quickly turned into a bad place whenever I showed up so I was always glad to give myself up and be sent back to approved school.

I didn't take any shit from anyone in approved school. Even the so-called big boys were wary of me. One character bashed my head against a brick wall seven times but I got my own back the very next day. But I never told anyone what Alex had done to me.

Then, towards the end of my sentence, I got called into the headmaster's office.

'You're going home,' he told me.

I was delighted but then I noticed the expression on his face and knew something was wrong. He told me Mum been raped and beaten up by Alex and that was why they were letting me go early.

I could feel the anger welling up inside me almost immediately. I was going to go straight to that bastard's house and finish him off for good. I saw myself getting hold of Alex and hitting him as hard as I could. All I could think about was what I was going to do to him for hurting Mum.

'Is my mum OK? Is my mum OK?' I kept asking the headmaster over and over again.

'Well, I've got her letter here in which she talks about what's happened.'

In that letter, she also said she'd gone to her local MP to ask for me to be allowed out early because of what had happened with Alex. Mum had moved out of the flat in Southampton after the attack and was now living in an area called Portswood.

After the headmaster read the letter to me, I burst into tears. 'I'll kill him. I'll kill him,' I kept on muttering.

'Take it easy, John,' said the headmaster, but they must have known revenge was in my heart.

Rape was a heavy word and it conjured up appalling images of physical violence in my mind and he had to pay for what he'd done, even though Mum had been too scared to press charges against Alex. I had two more weeks before my actual release and I could hardly sleep a wink. All I kept thinking about was that bastard Alex and how he would be made to pay for what he'd done to Mum.

When I finally got out, I headed straight round to our old home in Southampton. I had my bag with all my belongings clutched in my hand. I was even still wearing my grey flannel approved-school suit. I was like a kid possessed with only one intention – to get that animal once and for all.

I knocked on the door. No one answered at first so I tried harder. Eventually, he opened it. He tried to grease me with a slimy smile. 'Hello, John. How're you?'

I didn't say a word but laid a right-hander on him instantly. BOOM! He stood there for a moment in shock, holding his bleeding nose and I stupidly stood back. That's when he came back at me with a severe upper cut to the body. We then got in a big scrap on the doorstep. Alex seemed as strong as ever. At first, he definitely had the upper hand, which was hardly surprising considering he was a lot taller and broader than me. But I'd been training hard in approved school for this moment. Out of nowhere, I felt a burst of energy, probably fuelled by the sheer hatred I felt for this man who once called himself my dad. I knocked him flying to the ground with a flurry of punches. As he fell, his glasses dropped out of his pocket and I grabbed them.

'You're hurting me. You're hurting me,' muttered Alex, as I leaned down to finish him off.

'Hurting you? I'm gonna fuckin' kill ya! You don't touch my mum. Never.'

Then I crouched down and started hitting him even harder at close range. I was pummelling into him just the same way he'd pummelled me for so many years. I was shaking with rage, completely out of control and virtually unstoppable. The kid he'd once hit to within an inch of his life was now a fighting-fit youth who was more than a match for this bully. When I stopped punching him, Alex rolled over and started trying to crawl across the entrance to the flat we once lived in as a family. I kicked him and kicked him. Each time, his body collapsed to the ground before he once again painfully eased himself towards his home.

'Don't you ever, EVER touch my mum again! I'm the man in her life now! Look at me, you bastard. Look at me! You will never touch my mother again!'

Alex now looked like a terrified child. After so many painful battles, I'd won the war.

That afternoon, I went round to Mum's new place in Portswood and presented her with Alex's glasses. I told her, 'He'll never ever touch you again. I promise, Mum. He will never come near you again.'

I didn't care if Alex called the police on me, although I knew he wouldn't dare. I'd wanted to kill him at one stage but now I was glad he was still alive and knew that, if he dared make another move towards Mum, then he'd have me to contend with.

I never saw Alex again. Even when he came to see his son Andrew, he'd send in his new girlfriend to collect him from Mum's home rather than face me. He did once try to ring Mum. I made sure he was told in no uncertain terms never to contact her again. 'Keep looking over your shoulder because I'll be there. I'll hunt you down and find you. Don't ever ring this number again.'

I left home shortly after getting back from approved school and worked in a bakery in Portswood. It was a good job and I worked there until I was 20.

Nearly 20 years later, Andrew came to London to live with me, and Alex drove him to my flat in Notting Hill. When Andrew arrived, he knocked on the door and I opened the window and looked down at him.

'Hello, mate.'

'Can my dad use the toilet?'

'Tell him to go in the gutter. I never want him to talk to or see any of us ever again.'

That was it. I never actually saw him because he didn't dare get out of the car after he heard me shouting.

Mum and I never talked about Alex. She didn't even explain why she stayed with him for so long. I later heard he'd remarried and never laid a finger on his other children. I just don't understand why he went after me the way he did.

Mum eventually settled down with another man, who was also called Alex and came from Scotland. They even had a baby together. But there were no other similarities. I later told the bad Alex's son Andrew about what I'd done that day I got out of approved school and he said he would have done the same thing.

I heard from Andrew that Alex died a few years later from asbestos poisoning. Thank you, God. Thank you, God. I'm glad Alex died in pain and agony. He deserved it. I know I shouldn't think this way but, after the many batterings he gave me, I can't help myself.

Now I'm the father of three boys and I would never dream of hitting them. I survived being Alex's punchbag and I still have the scars on me to this day. His violence helped make me a very determined person and I've led a wonderfully varied and exciting life. I've met quite a few people who suffered similar abuse to me and I'm always struck by how remarkable it is that we've all moved on and made something out of our lives.

5

Anita

I WAS BORN in 1947 in leafy Walton-on-Thames, Surrey, and, until I was four and a half years old, we all lived at my grandparents' house. My first bad childhood memory is of the day we moved out of there, because I'd loved it so much at my nan's. My mum and dad were obviously desperate to get into their own home. At least it was only 15 minutes' walk from the council estate where Nan lived. I remember standing in my bedroom at my nan's on the morning of the move, with tears rolling down my face because I knew I wouldn't be sleeping there any more.

Life at my nan's had seemed so perfect. There were always lots of activities and people coming and going. It was a classic street where everyone knew everyone else. My memories of her home are like something out of one of those old black-and-white newsreels: lots of womenfolk in pinnies and men going off to work in their overalls, tipping their cloth caps to neighbours in the street.

We moved everything from my nan's by horse and cart that day in 1951 and I've never forgotten the shiver that went up my spine when the cart turned into this deathly quiet road which my dad said was where we were going to live. I was so disappointed. It seemed like an alien world. No one was out on the street. Everything was immaculate and it was a cul-de-sac so there wasn't even any flow of traffic. I demanded to be taken back to Nan's immediately but Mum and Dad both ignored me. I cried myself to sleep that night in my new home. I couldn't understand why Mum and Dad had changed everything.

Our new home was in a stuffy, private road and I didn't know where I belonged. I wanted to be back on the council estate where Nan lived, not this isolated piece of suburbia. As I got older, the other kids at school started saying I wasn't one of them any more because I lived in a posh area now. If only they realised how unlucky I felt. I promised myself that at every opportunity throughout my childhood I'd slip back to my nan's because it felt more like home than with my parents.

My father Graham was a boat-builder down on the

nearby Thames and my mum Doreen worked at a factory with her sisters and friends. I liked the fact they both worked because on school holidays I'd be walked to my nan's every day before they both went off to their jobs. My nan Jill would look after me and protect me along with my granddad Eric.

Dad started work at six or seven every morning and would finish at two and pick me up afterwards from Nan's. Every day, from the age of five, he'd take me to an athletics track after deciding I was going to be an Olympic runner. He'd first asked me if I wanted to be an ice skater or a runner and, because I'd always been scared of ice and falling over, I chose running.

Each day, I was taken to a different track to teach me how to deal with every type of environment. Nine Elms was windy, cold and exposed. There was the hot and humid indoor track at Tolworth, while the open-air one at Croydon had an extra-hard surface and was always crowded. Dad liked to make it as difficult as possible for me. And naturally, he bought all the relevant coaching books and manuals. Dad never did anything by halves. He was going to get me into the Olympics even if it killed him and I didn't have a lot of choice in the matter.

So, from the age of five, Dad would come into my bedroom on Saturday and Sunday mornings, often before it was even light, and get me up, saying he needed some peat for the garden from the woods at the end of the road. He always promised that we'd see some rabbits so I happily went along. I remember there'd often be this humid mist hanging over the woods, which made it quite creepy. I even recall being smaller than the ferns that sprouted everywhere but I don't think I ever actually saw any rabbits. We also never bumped into anyone else in the woods because it was so early. Dad used to go on about how it was the best time of the day to be there. I would have been terrified if he hadn't held my hand.

It's strange looking back on it, but I can't actually remember what happened when we got into the woods. I honestly don't know if I'm saying this because something bad did occur or not. I presume Dad found his precious peat and we walked back home together but it's all a bit of a blank now. Apparently, we went to those woods pretty regularly until I was about seven. But the running practice went on for many more years.

I haven't mentioned much about my mum so far because, for most of my childhood, she seemed like a distant figure, lurking in the background. She had six brothers and sisters and must have failed to get much attention as a child. Many years later, when I first went to therapy, the therapist said, 'So when did your mum die?' because there was no sense of her existence in my life, even though she's still very much alive and kicking to this day!

Mum and Dad were a good-looking couple who'd married very young and had me when they were not much more than 20 years old. They didn't have any more children because Mum said it was all too exhausting. Naturally, Dad had always wanted a boy, but in the end he had to make do with little me.

Dad was incredibly attentive towards me but that also meant he lost his temper quite a lot. He was always shouting at me during homework. He was the one at home in the afternoons because he finished work early and he was obsessed with me doing well at everything.

Dad was 5ft 11in with dark hair and big blue eyes. He seemed extremely handsome to me and he remained slim and fit throughout his life. Both my parents were non-smokers and Mum hardly ever drank alcohol because it gave her migraines. Meanwhile, Dad was so controlling that when he had a drink he was always extremely careful not to actually get drunk.

Mum was about 5ft 2in tall and petite with short, conveniently cut blonde hair. But there was always this tension and unhappiness beneath the surface with her. To be blunt about it, if she didn't have anything to worry or be hysterical about, then she was not happy. I didn't realise it back then when I was a child, but I suppose she was jealous of me because Dad chose to spend more time with me than her. It must have been tough on Mum.

Dad had served in Burma during the war and these days I suppose you'd call him a bit damaged by being in the thick of the fighting. He returned from Asia in 1946, the year before I was born, having gone off there aged just 18.

Everyone always used to say Dad was 'such a gentle giant' but actually he had the foulest temper. I knew it was there and lived in fear of it erupting. And my first real memory of it was one of those afternoons when he tried to teach me maths.

He'd be standing there constantly making sure I did my homework properly and criticising the teachers and insisting he would teach me correctly. Dad always knew best. He'd say I wasn't trying when I said I didn't understand something.

'Try harder.'

'I am trying, Dad.'

'You're not trying hard enough.'

Then he'd get really angry with me and storm out of the room. And I'd be the one mortified that I'd upset him. Those temper tantrums were very distressing: his eyes would flare up then he'd shake.

Then I'd notice him gritting his teeth and clenching his fists to avoid lashing out at me. He'd then let out a long, deep breath and storm off. Five minutes later, he'd return, having made the effort to calm down. Then he'd tell me all over again how to do the maths.

Holidays, however, were great fun when I was little. I remember when I was five we actually flew from Croydon Airport to North Wales to stay in a holiday camp. Mum and Dad were in their mid-twenties and I soon found things to do on my own. Typical only child I suppose. Anyway, I quickly made friends – with five grown men.

They were on their own in the holiday camp. I ended up spending loads of time in their chalet and Mum always laughs because she remembers sitting with Dad in the canteen when I came in with these five guys and said, 'That's my mum and dad over there but can I sit with you?'

I spent most of my holiday with these five men. I do not know even today if they were paedophiles or completely innocent but, looking back on it, it does seem strange that five men would stay in a family-style holiday camp. Dad even took a photo of them. Whenever I look at that photo, I come out in goose bumps because I keep wondering what their motives really were. Maybe I will never know. But I think it's fair to say Mum and Dad were pretty stupid to let me go and be with them when I was only five years old.

After that holiday, I became much more confident with adults and I often smiled and chatted with a middle-aged man who lived opposite our house. Then one day I knocked on his front door and said hello because he'd been nice to me in the street. Then he started inviting me into his house and even bought me a dress. It was salmon pink with a big, fluffy collar. I remember Mum put it on me so I looked good at her works Christmas do one year. This was very different from the men in the holiday camp because I have vivid memories of what happened with that neighbour and I know he hurt me. Today, I suppose, parents would be much more wary of a man like that, but back in those days they didn't give it a second thought.

This neighbour was quite old, in his forties, and I can't even remember his name to this day. He was only ever known as 'the neighbour' to me and my parents. I never saw any other children going in or out of his house but then there were no other children in our road. I do remember the lemon squash he always gave me with ice in it, which was quite a special treat back then. He also had a garden with a big cherry tree and a creepy-looking rundown shed at the far end. I don't even think 'the neighbour' had a car but I remember he always wore suits, which made him look very important and official. My dad only ever wore suits on special occasions.

But it's that dress he gave me which stands out most in my mind. It must have been a reward for something but I've wracked my brain for years and still can't come up with an answer. I think it might have been for my birthday in October and I do recall it came in a big posh white box. He gave it to me round at his house. He never once came into our house or got invited in. I took that box over the road and showed it off to Mum who was incredibly impressed and, as usual, never questioned his motives in giving me such an expensive gift.

My friendship with 'the neighbour' faded out in the end and I still don't really know what happened even now. My main memories are of him being a nice man but very smarmy. I also recall little white ankle socks, mine, as I sat on his knee. I feel more anger towards Dad for not working out that the neighbour was a bad person. As for Mum – how could I have high expectations of someone so obsessed by herself?

Mum encouraged me to wear that dress for a long time afterwards and it was even handed down to my cousin Fiona. For some reason, I disassociated it from what had happened to me. The main image I recall about that house was the darkness. There were no bookshelves. Everything seemed so bare. I don't even recall a telly. But there was a musty, rotting-food type of smell. I did later hear that his mother had died in that front room some years earlier.

Many times since then I've had a recurring nightmare about that house. It's always in flames and there's this old-fashioned telephone and I'm putting my fingers in the dial but they keep slipping out and I can't get the phone to work and I also can't seem to get away. I don't know if he even had a phone in real life. Maybe that phone was a symbol for something else.

Back at home, Dad made learning how to ride a bike incredibly stressful. When I didn't get it straight away, he got angry with me. Learning to run fast was fine because I'd managed that instantly. I suppose you could say he was the classic type of father of a budding sports star. He was a fanatical parent, determined to make his child succeed in all the areas where, I presume, he'd failed. It meant there was little room for error.

Dad wouldn't even allow me to have stabilisers to stop me falling off my bike when he taught me how to ride. I'd got my bicycle on Christmas Day and I was so happy but then Dad got angry with me for not managing to ride it instantly up and down the road outside our home. I wobbled all over the place and then put my feet down to balance myself. As I've said, I was always petrified of falling, which made it even more frightening.

'KEEP YER FEET ON THE PEDALS, GIRL!' Dad screamed at me, as if the future of the world depended on it.

After going around the block about a dozen times, I finally got the hang of it and the pressure was off. I felt it, even back then.

I can't remember where Mum was that Christmas morning. Mind you, most Christmas mornings, she'd be lying in bed suffering from some ailment or other. Usually, the curtains were drawn because of her migraine. The only conversations I remember having with Mum as a child were about food and diet. She wasn't the most communicative mother in the world, although she did frequently point out that Dad's side of the family had weight problems. Mum made my Dad fat-phobic, which is why they're so slim even now. Dad's mother was known as the local fat lady and his sisters were all fat and pregnant by 15, so there was no way his daughter was going to turn out like that.

The only time I could stuff my face properly was when I went to my lovely nan's for lunch. Thank God for Nan's — it was like a refuge from the boring, fat-free life I was leading with my parents.

But then, when I was about nine, it stopped being so great at my nan's. I was still being dropped off there most days before Mum or Dad picked me up after work. Nan's youngest son Greg – my mother's youngest brother – was 15 or 16 at the time and still living at home. He had a job at the local garage and used to get every Wednesday afternoon off. Uncle Greg – with his blond hair – was very good-looking in a James Dean kind of way. One Wednesday, I arrived at Nan's to find that Uncle Greg had built me a swing in the back garden. I was delighted. But he was soon pushing me so hard on that swing that I felt I was about to fall and I hated that feeling. So I begged him to stop but he just ignored me and kept going.

Finally, he slowed down and grabbed one of my arms and legs and spun me around and around like an aeroplane until I was really giddy and then dropped me on the grass where he tickled me until I virtually wet myself. We went through the same ritual for many Wednesdays until a few months later when he picked me up from the grass and carried me to Nan's outside toilet. I remember the apple tree next to it because, when he started touching me, I closed my eyes and I could smell the pungent aroma of the mouldy apples, which he'd stepped through to get to that toilet. I can't talk about the rest because it's too horrible to think about, even today. He took my innocence from me.

I never told a soul what happened. Just the thought of Mum knowing what her brother did to me made me feel very scared. In any case, no one would have believed the word of a scatty little nine-year-old girl. It went on for months and, not surprisingly, completely changed my attitude towards my beloved nan's house. It had gone from the best place in the world to the worst virtually overnight. But, because I didn't tell my parents, they kept dropping me there every day before going to work. Uncle Greg had created an environment that enabled him to do anything he wanted to me.

Now I just have these brief, blurry images that occasionally go through my head when I think about what he did to me:

Back garden.

Swing.

Apple tree.

Toilet.

Over and over and over again:

Back garden.

Swing.

Apple tree.

Toilet.

Nan didn't have a clue what was happening. I think

she was often in a neighbour's house having a cup of tea. It must have all sounded like good, clean fun as Uncle Greg swung me around and around. No one told him to stop. No one stepped into the garden and said, 'Enough is enough.' Everyone else just thought it was all a good laugh. My auntie Janet was living in Nan's house at the time with her husband and little girl. But none of them even noticed.

Uncle Greg took me into this horrible, painful world, which ended in him doing things to me in the outside loo. After that first time, he just opened the door and in we would go. But you know what? Until he started hurting me, he'd been my favourite person. I'd already learned that I had to please my father so it seemed natural to please Uncle Greg as well, which is perhaps why I allowed him to take me into the outside toilet in the first place.

Uncle Greg never hit me or threatened me. It was the tickling and the giddiness that broke down my defences. He wore me down until he knew I was in a vulnerable state. The time between when I first got on the swing and that walk to the toilet was usually quite long. He built it all up carefully and cynically.

After he'd done those mean, horrible things to me, I'd stay and have tea at my nan's until Dad came to pick me up. I'd be close to tears and unable to eat anything but no one in that house even asked me what was wrong. Then Dad would take me off for more bloody running. It was the last thing I needed. What I really wanted was someone to talk to about what had happened.

Now I know better, I can say without doubt that I compartmentalised what Uncle Greg did to me so everything else carried on as normal in my life. Uncle Greg only stopped when he got a girlfriend. He never talked to me about it, even though we've seen each other many times since at family parties and gatherings.

Once he left my nan's place, it all went back to being good again, although it would never be quite the same. I was still a jolly, bright, fun-loving child who adored school and had a great circle of friends but I hated going home to Mum and Dad's because it was so empty.

In the evenings, I had to change my personality and become this quiet, reserved proper little girl who did what she was told and rarely answered back. At home, I spent most of my time in my room alone except when Dad came in to have a go at me about my homework. Besides the pressure of running practice, he was also piling on the pressure for me to pass my eleven-plus exams.

As I got older, Dad's temper certainly worsened. One day I was with a friend called Terry in Dad's new

Austin A-7 car when he cut someone up en route to athletics practice. The other driver chased us up the road and stopped his car right in front of Dad. Dad was infuriated, and he got out of the car, ran up to this bloke and punched him so hard in the face that he fell over. Both me and Terry sitting in the back of the car were speechless. It was the only time I ever actually saw Dad lose it in public. He immediately got back in the car, said 'Sorry about that' and on we went. It was never mentioned again.

Dad definitely took the running more seriously than me. One time, we were staying in Blackpool for the school athletics championships. Mum was sick as usual and back in the hotel, lying in bed, so Dad let me go off to the funfair on my own with some friends. There were trams in Blackpool and Dad arranged to pick me up from the tram-stop on my return from the fair. At the funfair, the trams were all so full I waited an hour to get a place on one. Anyway, I was late for Dad and when I explained that the trams were all full he didn't believe me.

'Your mum's ill. She's worried sick and you lie to me?'

Then – WHACK! – I got a thump round the back of the head.

He then grabbed my arm and dragged me back into the hotel. We had a meal in silence that night with Mum still in bed in their room. He did eventually say sorry, but not until the next day.

Then Dad got a motorbike and built a wooden sidecar for me, which looked more like a small boat. I hated being driven around in that embarrassing sidecar. Mum remained this distant figure in the background, either tucked up in bed or hovering in the kitchen.

Meanwhile, Uncle Greg remained a constant reminder of those awful incidents in the toilet at Nan's place. I was even bridesmaid at his wedding a couple of years later when he was 18. He gave me a special present as a 'thank you'. I suppose it was to keep me quiet about what had happened.

Down the years, Uncle Greg has continued to repulse me by always greeting me with a kiss on the lips. He was and still is very tactile. I suppose back then he was what we'd call a groper but these days they're better known as groomers. Everyone always thought Uncle Greg was such a good laugh. If only they knew the truth. He's still married today, with three children and seven grandchildren.

Dad never once picked up on what happened with Uncle Greg. He was more concerned with my future as an Olympic runner. Then I went and broke my arm doing the high jump at school. Dad ignored it at first and told me it was nothing but a sprain, and he took me to training later that same day. But my coach immediately realised what had happened to my arm and got very angry with Dad for bringing me running. Dad was furious at me for getting injured and I remember his face went black with rage when the doctor at the hospital held the x-ray up to show him the break. It was the same face Dad used during maths homework. I'd let him down again.

My arm was put in plaster in the hospital, but Dad still took me running the following day and even made me put a sock and plastic bag over the plaster so it wouldn't get wet. However, Dad was very careful not to take me to our usual club because he knew that the coach would have a go at him.

My father's overprotectiveness and control over me remains the biggest single influence on my childhood. As a result, I became a rebel in my early teens. I'd broken my arm and then started to put on a bit of weight – two things Dad definitely wasn't happy about. Then Mum started trying to put me on diets under Dad's supervision. He even made me drink this dreadful wheat stuff called Beemax. They gave me special packed lunches for school that consisted of unbuttered sandwiches and dry fruit. Thank god for Nan's – I still relished slipping back there for a wonderful fatty meat and two veg. She was a great cook in the old-fashioned sense of the word. And Uncle Greg was long gone.

I soon gave up running completely after that injury and Dad replaced it in his life by playing football and then managing a local football team. He became equally obsessive about that. I suppose the football team was just another version of me. I heard he was a hard coach to please.

After years of pleasing Dad all the time, I went completely the other way. One day, Dad turned up with his bloody motorcycle sidecar to pick me up from school and I slipped out the other entrance so he didn't see me. Then I went and met some boys on the common. I told Dad I'd gone straight to an extra art class and he rang the school to see if I was lying. He was furious when he found out no such thing existed. But I didn't care by then.

I was a real leader in school and hated bullying and, if anyone tried to push my classmates around, I'd sort it out immediately. People thought I was a bit of a hard nut but I wasn't really.

When I was 13, I went to Battersea funfair with my old running friend Jane, who was much more grown up than me. She was from south London and had older brothers and sisters, while I was this much less experienced girl from the sleepy lanes of Surrey. Jane had been to the fair quite a few times before and even knew the boys running the bumper cars. She fancied one of them and he and his mate offered to walk us across Battersea Park to the nearest bus stop. And naive little me thought that was all they intended to do.

Sex still petrified me and I used to listen in awe to all the girls at school bragging about what they'd done with boys. Those incidents with Uncle Greg and that neighbour had been slotted into another compartment of my brain and I was many, many years away from even attempting to deal with them.

So, back at Battersea funfair, we let these two boys – I suppose they were about 18 – walk us through the park. Then Jane and her fella stopped by a bench. Naively, I asked her what was happening because I didn't want to be late for the bus. Then this other boy said to me, 'Come on,' and he assumed we were going to have a bit of fun behind a bush. Both boys seemed very scary to me. Anyway, we sat down on this bench and he put his hand up my skirt and I started to panic because I was desperate to stop him touching me. In the end, he got very annoyed and virtually ordered me to masturbate him, but I didn't know how to do it so he showed me. That then became the pattern for me with boys when I was in my early teens. I would do things for them so they wouldn't touch me.

Subconsciously I was dealing with those attacks on

me when I was younger. I didn't want the same thing to happen to me so I became an expert at satisfying boys without letting them actually touch me.

One time when I was 14 or 15, I was supposed to be staying at a friend's house before going straight to school the next day. Then I met this boy on a bus and decided to take him with me and my friend to a youth club that evening. We were having a snog outside when Dad decided to drive by on his silly motorbike to make sure I was behaving and that the youth club was suitable. I was in the middle of my kiss and cuddle when I felt this stinging pain, as a hand whacked me across the back of the head. The boy was terrified when he saw Dad standing there. Dad took me home and tried to stop me going out for the next month. He made me feel as if I'd committed a cardinal sin.

Now in my mid-teens, trouble seemed to follow me everywhere. I'd get myself into stupid situations before I realised what was happening. Once, I found myself in a car with a bloke who'd driven me down this isolated towpath by the river. I demanded he take me home because I was so upset that he wanted to have sex with me.

Other children's parents started to take pity on me because I was so lonely at home. One mum even gave me a book about teenage sex and had a right go at my own mum because she felt I'd been neglected. Mum was furious, but I think she knew this other woman was right. Mum never even talked to me about sex until I was 17, and then she told me not to bother doing it because 'it's not very nice'.

Dad couldn't cope with the idea of me having sex, so he found it even harder to deal with all the things that happened to me around the ages of 14 or 15. I think he gave up on me in the end. In his eyes, I was a failure who hadn't made the Olympic athletics team, which was why he went off and coached that football team. I didn't get as many O levels as he wanted me to either. I desperately wanted to go to art college, but he wouldn't let me because he said it was full of druggies. 'You have to go straight to work,' he said. I actually wanted to be a policewoman and eventually became a fingerprint technician at Scotland Yard, which was the same rank as a constable.

I was still living at home when I got pregnant by a boy called Dave whom my parents naturally couldn't stand. They were actually right to hate him because he turned out to be a very violent character. After marrying Dave, we lived as a couple at my parents' house and had the baby, which turned out to be the boy Dad had so desperately wanted. Eventually, they kicked my violent husband out but expected me and the baby to stay. But when I told Dad I loved Dave and would have to go with him, Dad said, 'What about me? Don't I deserve some consideration?'

Dave and I eventually split up and then divorced.

He was actually murdered a long time after we divorced, although it's hard to feel sorry for him because he was very violent towards me and battered me. One time, he broke my jaw. Later, when he saw me with a new boyfriend, he nearly killed the poor bloke.

When I was in my twenties, I asked my younger cousin Sally if Uncle Greg had ever touched her. She was so annoyed by my question that I couldn't admit what had happened to me. There was also another pretty young girl relative who I think Uncle Greg tried to do things to. She became very anorexic and I wondered if it was because of Uncle Greg. I even attended a family Christmas party when this girl got very drunk and seemed very upset. I eventually got her treated for anorexia in hospital. It later emerged that she had been sexually abused and I said I thought I knew who'd done it because he'd done it to me.

She just looked at me and said, 'I am not talking about it.'

Then I said, 'It's Uncle Greg, isn't it?'

She just burst into tears. She never said who it was, but I know it was him.

I've never sought revenge against Uncle Greg because I'm still the sort of person who'd rather let sleeping dogs lie. I am not good at confrontations. People have got away with so many things against me all through my life and I've done nothing about it. Sometimes I think to myself, That's really out of order. Why haven't I gone mad about that? But I just don't. It's not the way I am.

But I am angry about what Uncle Greg did to that other relative and he deserves to be put away. But nobody would have believed my word against Uncle Greg. Everyone, even today, keeps saying how Uncle Greg has the perfect marriage and what a great bloke he is. We even hear about what a great sex life he and his wife Pamela have. Mum still adores Uncle Greg and so does Dad. If only they knew.

I do sometimes have little fantasies about Uncle Greg's funeral. I think about how, when everyone's weeping, I'll be laughing. He is a deeply disturbed man who deserves no sympathy. He probably doesn't even see himself as a paedophile, yet I'm certain he's interfered with other children. A few years ago, Uncle Greg had to have a heart bypass operation so maybe that means he feels bad about what he's done.

This might sound weird, but, if Uncle Greg was outside my flat standing on the balcony threatening to jump, I wouldn't stop him. I hope he dies sooner rather than later. But, before he jumped, I'd want to know why he'd felt the urge to hurt me and others in the first place.

In the late 1980s, I trained to be a therapist for three years and worked in a home for battered women as well as a place for women sexually abused in their childhood. Then I went to work at a clinic in London, which included 18 months on the psychiatric wards. I have come across many versions of myself in these places.

A few years back, I had a pivotal moment with my father after a lifetime of his being in control. Dad had bought this book about the last war and he started talking about it. He'd hardly mentioned the war to me before. It turned out Dad's platoon was hit by friendly fire from the Allies. Only about seven of his mates made it across this hill. Dad passed me this book he'd bought and told me to read a specific chapter about that incident. He remained sitting next to me as I was reading and then I noticed he was crying. He couldn't talk because he was so upset and I put my hand on his and said, 'It's all right, Dad.' It was the first time I felt stronger than him. It was a really powerful, liberating moment for me.

Now there is an equal balance between us. Now he talks about the war all the time. He's opened up for the first time in his life. After retirement, Dad made a special effort to nurture my son and they've been close ever since he was a small child.

So I've finally sorted out these issues from my childhood and my life has become so much more settled. I live in a beautiful apartment and enjoy my life more than I ever thought was possible. I know I've suffered but not nearly as much as many other people. We have to learn to deal with the past while always keeping an eye on the future. Despite everything, I wouldn't swap my life with anyone else.

6

Graham

MY NAME IS Graham Johnson and I was born in 1953 in Fulham, west London. I was the first child of three brothers. My childhood abuse started and ended with being beaten to a pulp by my father. The first time it happened I was four or five years old, but from then on I was assaulted by him virtually every single day. Sometimes the beatings were especially vicious but, even now, I still can't remember why they were worse on certain occasions. It's almost as if the sheer physical nature of my dad's attacks forced my mind to block them out. It was just easier to deal with them that way.

We were very poor during my early childhood. My dad was a strong, solitary figure who'd been quite a hero during the war on the Royal Navy MTB

(Motor Torpedo Boats), which patrolled off the coast of Norfolk. He risked being blown sky high every time his boat went out to sea, but by all accounts he coped admirably, although I think he came home a changed man, like so many who served in those two world wars.

Dad's name was Harold and he was Fulham born and bred, just like me. We even went to the same school. In fact, maybe that was the root of many of our problems – we were incredibly alike. My mum Rose was an East End girl. She enjoyed being looked after by Dad and he certainly ruled the waves at home from the day they got married.

Mum and Dad were like so many couples who met and fell in love shortly after the war. They were all looking for peace and security after suffering appalling hardship. People like my parents probably tried too hard, which might be why Dad felt under so much pressure to provide for his family. I've always wondered if that's why he took out so many of his frustrations on me.

I'll never forget the very first beating I suffered. I was five years old at the time and we'd moved a few miles west to a house on Munster Road, in Fulham. Dad used to go to work at the crack of dawn every day, and each morning Mum would take me out of the house and we'd walk around the streets of west

London looking in the shops or playing in the park. Later, I found out the reason she did this was to save on the electricity and gas bills. That was a measure of how poor we were. Every penny counted back then. One day, Mum took me to Woolworths in North End Road and then to the Lyons Corner House where we had a bun and a cup of tea.

Dad was an electrician on the London Underground network. He'd finish work at about 1pm and then go to the pub for a couple of hours before arriving home at about four or five for his tea. But on this particular day he was in a foul mood, especially when he found out Mum had dared to spend a few pennies on a bun and a cuppa.

I guess that's why he sent me flying across the room when he hit me across the head. I don't know why he picked on me that day or on any of the hundreds and hundreds of occasions after that. All I know is that from that moment onwards my childhood became a living nightmare. At some point most afternoons or evenings, I was going to get smashed to bits by my old man.

After Dad hit me that first time, I cried and rushed into the kitchen where Mum was standing. She tried to console me but only whispered a few words in case Dad got even angrier when he heard her talk to me. I didn't dare ask why he'd hit me in the first place.

The beatings got much more severe when my brother Gordon was born just after my fifth birthday. Looking back on it, I suppose Dad was under even more financial pressure because he'd had another child and he needed an outlet for his frustration. But I'm no expert so you can draw your own conclusions. All I do know is that there was a tremendous amount of pressure on us.

But, as far as I am aware, Dad never lifted a finger to Mum or my brother at that time. Meanwhile, my punishments were turning into a virtual nightly occurrence.

It's difficult not to cry when I think back to what I suffered at Dad's hands. I remember he began using this big stick, which he leaned against the wall in the corner of the hallway of our tiny home. Really, it was nothing more than a bit of two-by-two wood that was about four feet in length.

The first time he used it was after he came home a bit the worse for drink and told Mum to send me to their bedroom and wait there. I didn't know what was going on at first but I was an obedient child so I went to the bedroom and waited for Dad to come in. I thought he was just going to give me a talking to, or some sort of bollocking.

When he finally walked in and I saw the stick in his hand, I knew I was going to get hurt so I simply bent over the bed and waited for the inevitable. He didn't utter a word before smashing the corner of that piece of two-by-two across my thighs and arse. I don't recall exactly how many times he hit me in the bedroom that day but I gritted my teeth and took the punishment. Once he'd left the room, I slipped out and headed for Mum in the kitchen. But, as usual, she was afraid to give me any real love or affection in case Dad got even more angry because she'd dared to console me.

Later on, being in that bedroom waiting for his stick became a more painful form of punishment than the actual beatings because I'd wait there sometimes for hours knowing that I was going to get hurt. I'm crying now just thinking back to the fear and trepidation I felt all alone in that bedroom. Often, I'd lie face down on the bed immediately after walking in because I didn't want to see Dad's face when he entered the room. It seemed easier to cope with the punishments if they just came out of nowhere. It could be ten minutes or two hours. It was never the same amount of time. I'd be shaking like a leaf by the time he walked in. Looking back on it, I wonder if he got some sort of perverse pleasure out of mentally torturing me.

The worst thing was I'd never know how many times he was going to hit me. It was always on the arse and top of the legs. The only thing I remember Mum sometimes saying to Dad when he sent me to the bedroom was: 'Don't hit him on the head.'

Mum did absolutely nothing to stop Dad's attacks. She was totally under his control. He had a physical and mental hold over her. Mind you, Dad wasn't someone to have a row with. He was six foot tall and had a 44-inch chest. He was also a black belt in judo and had nearly represented Britain in the Commonwealth Games. You just didn't fuck with my dad. He'd take on all comers and beat them. He was a scary fella to meet down a dark alley and he certainly wasn't afraid of anyone.

When I was about six, we moved yet again. But nothing much else changed in my miserable childhood. Dad still got up early for work, popped in the boozer every afternoon then rolled in pissed before lashing out at me.

We did very little together like a normal father and son. I cannot remember any Christmases in my childhood. It's all just a blank. If you asked me what was my normal Christmas Day, I wouldn't be able to tell you.

I went to hospital at least ten times after being beaten by my father. No one ever asked me how I got my injuries and the police were never involved. I usually went to the Fulham Hospital in Fulham

Palace Road and no one mentioned the fact I'd been in there many times before. I regularly stayed overnight and Dad never once came to visit me.

He didn't even have to tell me not to say anything. He just knew that I'd keep quiet. I got a couple of visits from Mum but she'd never talk about what had happened. His beatings became an unmentionable subject.

The only time I ever remember Dad actually bothering to tell me why he was beating me to a pulp occurred on what should have been one of the happiest days of my childhood. It's difficult to recall it without sobbing at the sheer brutality of what happened.

Let me explain. I was at a school in Fulham and worked very hard at my classes and sport. I preferred it to home for obvious reasons. Anyway, I'd been to the school presentation day where we all got gongs and stuff, and me and my two best classmates Dave and Brian were pretty elated after a wonderful day of happiness. I remember it was a cold, wet November day and the three of us were walking home along a quiet side street singing 'God Save The Queen'. We weren't drunk. We weren't being rude to passers-by. We were just in high spirits like 13-year-old kids often are.

Anyway, this Old Bill (policeman) stopped us on

the pavement near our homes and demanded to know what we were doing, as if it was against the law to be happy. When we laughed and explained we were just coming home from a school prize-giving, this big bastard of a copper clumped me right across the head. It really hurt, but my two mates were reluctant to intervene in case we all got nicked. Then this same copper gives me another clump before telling us all to 'fuck off home and keep the noise down'.

I got home about ten minutes later with this big swelling on the side of my face where that copper had hit me. Dad looked up from his tea and scowled at me. 'What you been doing?'

'Some copper hit me, Dad.'

Then he looked at me and said, 'You must have been in the wrong.'

'No, Dad. We were just walkin' home.'

'Bollocks,' he spat, getting up from his chair.

I knew exactly what was coming next, although it brings tears to my eyes to talk about it now. He walked right up to me and gave me a bash across the head followed by another crack for good measure.

That was the only time I ever knew why he hit me.

Later that day, Mum told me I had to go to the bedroom to wait for Dad. I knew what was coming. That stick left welts across my thighs as he smashed it down on me over and over and over again.

The only break in the endless brutality came when we went on holiday because Dad was actually a very adventurous traveller. I adored these trips because they broke the cycle of violence. He never hit me when we were on our travels. It was as if a different environment brought out a different character. One time, we went to the Black Forest, in Germany, and he even played with us and we shared a picnic. I've never forgotten it because it was such a rare occurrence. Abroad really was a different world.

Naturally, I used to dread holidays coming to an end because it always meant I'd be back on that conveyor belt of violence. And undoubtedly I soon inherited Dad's aggression. By my early teens, if people upset me I'd go and hunt them down and do them, just like he did me, because I thought that was normal. It was how I was brought up. Thank God, I never ever hit my own three kids later in life.

We never had meals together as a proper family. There was no small talk either. Dad simply ate his tea in silence and Mum did likewise. He never mentioned work and it seems strange to think I later went into the same business, even though I knew so little about it.

Every Friday afternoon, he'd come in from work – via the pub – with these envelopes. He'd give them to Mum and each one was marked 'rent', 'electric', 'telephone', 'gas' or 'food'. Inside was the money for each bill. It was a ritual of meanness because he wanted to control every penny that went in and out of our home.

Dad eventually started working as a black-cab driver in his spare time so that as we got older we wouldn't go so short of things. I inherited that same work ethic and had a paper round and worked for a fruit and vegetable merchant in Pimlico. Every Saturday, I delivered fruit and veg to the actress Honor Blackman and she was so pleasant to me. She was the nicest lady I ever met. I wasn't used to people treating me with genuine kindness.

But there are many more bad memories associated with the violence inflicted by my father. One time, I was in a bed in a children's hospital ward after yet another beating and I was feeling pretty sorry for myself. Then the matron came round and asked all the kids if they wanted to buy some sweets from a trolley in the hallway. They all got up and left the ward but I didn't have a penny to spend. I just lay there in tears because I realised then that my parents had virtually abandoned me. They never left me any money and no one even came in to see me during the five days I was in hospital.

There were other examples of neglect. I remember climbing on the back of a milkfloat and cutting my knee on a broken bottle. It was badly gashed and bleeding and I was in a right state. But, when I ran into the house with blood spurting in all directions, Mum wouldn't take me to the hospital because Dad was due home later that afternoon and he expected her to be there with his tea.

In the end, a neighbour called Peg rang for a cab and took me to the hospital. I was immediately admitted and stayed there for two or three days. That neighbour even paid for the cab herself and my parents never once came to see me. I still have the scar to this day. Mum put my father ahead of my health and safety. That was a measure of either her stupidity or her fear of him. Many years later, I collapsed round at her house with a mystery virus and she did exactly the same thing and let me make my own way to hospital, and you know what? She never even came to see me then, either.

Looking back on it, I don't think Dad ever mellowed out. He would start a punch-up at the drop of a hat, didn't matter what the situation was. Now I realise that everything in his life was confrontational. Mum had little option. If we were out, she had to get back before he returned from work. I never really had a proper conversation with my dad, otherwise perhaps we would have addressed these issues.

Dad liked everything to be regimented. On

Saturdays, Mum would go and see her mum in the East End and Dad would stay at home to look after us. Every Saturday morning, he'd come bounding into our bedroom and wake us up like a sergeant major by yelling, 'It's nine o'clock – all get up NOW!'

If, by a minute past nine, I wasn't up, then he grabbed all my bedclothes including a duvet, blanket and pillows and then opened the bedroom window and threw them out. Often he'd throw my clothes out as well. We were living three floors up in a block of flats at the time.

'Now make yer bed! Get down there and get it back!' he'd scream at me.

I'd then have to go down and apologise to the neighbour whose garden my bedclothes were in, grab them and then rush back upstairs to make my bed.

That was the way it was. As I got older and a little bit more defiant, he'd snap at me, 'If you don't like it, you can fuck off.' Ever since then, the first thing I do when I wake up every morning is make my bed, wherever I am sleeping.

And still Mum's only real words of tender loving care before the old man started bashing that stick down on me would be:

Don't hit him on the head.
Don't hit him on the head.
Don't hit him on the head.

I still don't know to this day why she couldn't have actually stood up for me. Her child. Her boy. She just didn't have the guts.

Dad was a handsome fellow but beneath those dark, swarthy good looks lay a man in turmoil. He was incredibly prejudiced against other creeds and colours. He wouldn't even let Mum on a bus if there was a black person already on it. I wish I knew where all this hatred came from.

Then Dad started targeting my middle brother Gordon for a few of his special punishments. He was only six or seven at the time. Gordon was a very different character from me and initially he dealt with Dad's violence by trying to run away from home.

Each time, he was rescued and brought home but he'd disappear again if my Dad laid another finger on him. It was disturbing to witness, but the rest of us were too scared of Dad to try to stop him. Unlike me, Gordon wasn't able to soak up the punishments. In some ways, I admired him for responding and seeking out answers to why it was happening.

Dad always kept a photo of Gordon upside down in a dustbin, which he thought was hilarious. He'd picked Gordon up when he was five or six and dropped him headfirst into a dustbin full of stinking, rotting rubbish when we were out at a pub for a family drink. That dustbin was filled with wasps and bees and other shit and Gordon was terrified and crying. But, instead of pulling my brother out, Dad looked down at him and said, 'Right, he can fuckin' stay there.'

As usual, Mum didn't utter a word. Gordon continued screaming and crying but Dad just turned away and went back to supping his pint. Other people in the pub garden were shocked. Dad didn't pull him out of there for another five minutes.

When Gordon turned seven, he twice took an overdose of pills. The first time, he was rushed to Fulham Hospital to have his stomach pumped. Within a week, he did it again. Dad was arrested on the second occasion for neglect, because the police said he should have removed all the pills from our home but he hadn't bothered because he refused to take Gordon's behaviour seriously. No one ever questioned Dad about why Gordon was trying to kill himself at such an incredibly young age.

Gordon took a big bashing after he got back from hospital for causing all this trouble. Mum did nothing as usual.

Another time – two or three years later – Dad's furious temper flared up in public in a way none of us has ever forgotten. We were in Devon on holiday. I must have been in my early teens, Gordon was eight or nine. We were having a great time, as we always did on holidays. We were in a place called Saltash, in Cornwall, and this bee stung my brother. Then this bloke sitting nearby turned towards us, as Dad was trying to calm Gordon down and said in a broad West Country accent, 'Lucky that's not one of my bees.' He was trying to make a joke of it.

Well, Dad's face turned to thunder, and he got up and smashed this bloke full on in the face. There's me, Mum and Gordon and all these people looking at my dad as if he's a complete nutter. He didn't say a word and sat back at our table and finished off his pint before announcing we should be on our way. That incident was never mentioned again.

But I was soon to be once again the sole recipient of Dad's violence. He still usually kept the attacks to within the four walls of our home, so none of my friends ever witnessed the beatings. In some ways, I suppose it was a bit like being at school the way he meted out his punishments. And I continued to bottle it all up and never told a soul what was happening. Back in those days, we still had corporal punishment in school. But, when I got home, there were much worse beatings awaiting me. And it seemed a lot more frightening than at school.

The strange thing is that no one ever questioned my injuries, even though I was often covered in bruises on my legs and backside. Throughout my childhood, Dad remained this incredibly solitary figure. He'd been one of 11 children – with five brothers and five sisters. Yet he never visited any of them. Dad had a few mates down the pub but he never brought anyone home. That would have affected his ability to choose when and where he wanted to hit me. I just wish I knew why. There was no respite for me. Maybe I was a bad person who deserved all this hatred.

One of the worst beatings I can remember was when I came home from school aged about 14 and Mum said, 'Go to the bedroom.' I still had on my school uniform of shorts and blazer and she said, 'Put yer long trousers on.'

I don't have a clue why he hit me that day. I wasn't that bad a kid and I certainly didn't deserve to be beaten so often. I vividly remember waiting in the bedroom that day. I kept hearing noises down the corridor but no one came for what seemed like hours. Eventually, Dad came in the room and I'd literally shat myself with fear because I knew something really bad was coming. He didn't bother hitting me because of the mess. I actually started to wonder if I should shit my pants every time, then he might not hit me.

Then he customised his very own punishment stick by adding bristles like on a clothes brush halfway down it. I'd get a certain side depending on what I'd done wrong. As usual, I'd lie across the bed face down, arse up waiting for it. Whatever comes, comes, I used to think to myself. I'd grit my teeth and try to convince myself I didn't care. I suppose I'd already been neutralised by the sheer number of beatings. Just get it over and done with. Please. So he'd come in, pick up the dreaded stick and hit me with all his strength.

He did hit me in public once when we went out as a family for a drink on a Sunday at a local pub with Dad's brother and his kids. It was a family afternoon treat and should have been a happy occasion. They had the old drinking laws back then, which meant all kids had to stay outside the pub. So Dad sat me down nearby and told me in front of the rest of the family, 'If you move, I'm gonna hit you. Just sit there quietly.' It was always said in an indifferent tone. I accepted it all without responding, as usual. Inside, I'd been emotionally dead for years.

I knew he'd come out and get me if I'd dared to move. But I couldn't resist playing tag with my cousin, and Dad spotted me through the window and came charging out like a madman and BANG! I got a clump. No word of explanation, but at least this time I knew the reason why.

Those sorts of attacks were nearly always across the

head. He called them 'perfect head shots'. None of my relatives would dare to interfere. Dad was not someone to be messed with. Just let him get on with it, they must have thought to themselves. If only they hadn't.

When I was 15, violence erupted under very different circumstances. Me and Dad and the rest of the family were in the garden of a pub together when these five quite meaty-looking blokes tried to chat up Mum. Dad was incensed and, after watching them for a few minutes, he said to me, 'They're taking the piss and we're gonna teach them a lesson, son. It's you and me.'

My mother looked frightened when she heard Dad. She knew how mindless his violence could be. Meanwhile, he kept saying, 'We're going to do them, boy. Come on. Let's get stuck in.'

So we had this almighty tear-up and laid into these blokes. Looking back on it, I realise we behaved like animals. But somehow the two of us smashed these guys up. And you know what? Afterwards, I felt so good. It was like a bonding thing between me and my dad. We'd won against all the odds. Maybe I'd even got a little smidgen of approval from him for the first time in my life. But he soon put me right by giving me a beating the next day, as usual for no good reason.

My biggest turning point came when I was 16. I was now six foot tall, spoke little and had become hardened to violence. The soul had been beaten out of me in emotional terms. I suppose I must have seemed quite a cold, indifferent kind of character. I'd even started hanging around with a load of fellas older than me, aged 18 to 20. They were nasty, hard cases but I loved being in their company because it gave me a sense of belonging.

We often went out to nightclubs in the West End. I was now physically much stronger and I soon got a reputation for not taking any shit. We got into quite a few scraps and I proved to the older chaps that I was a kid with a lot of bottle. I was still living at home and those experiences made me decide I wouldn't take any more shit off my old man.

One day, I walked in the front door to find him having a vicious argument with Mum. It was the first and only time I ever saw him raise a hand to her. I wasn't having any of that so I steamed into him and broke it up and we ended up having a stand-off. We stood facing each other waiting for the other to make the first move. I knew he probably could still have beaten me to death but I stood up to him and held my ground. We were the same height by now, although he still had a much bigger build.

We must have stood there for five minutes waiting to make our next moves and, for the first time in my life, I saw a look of hesitation on his face. He was weighing up his options, something he'd never done throughout all those previous childhood beatings. I was fed up with always being the victim. I was going to hit him back if necessary.

When he then took a deep breath, I thought that would spark the violence within him, but instead he just turned around and walked out of the flat to cool off. But, typically, Mum didn't say one word of thanks. It was almost as if she hadn't wanted me to save her. She was more terrified I'd upset my father.

Dad stopped hitting me after that, even though he was still probably more than capable of breaking my back in one quick judo move. We never talked about what happened that day or the beatings that occurred throughout so much of my childhood.

I left home after I got married at 23. Dad still had the same job as an electrician on the London Underground. I'd also joined the Underground after leaving school at 16.

The hours were good with an early start and an early finish. I even went to the pub for two hours at the end of each day just like he did. I initially worked for the Underground as an apprentice engineer just like my dad, even down to the four-year apprenticeship I served. I suppose it is significant that I followed my father's life so closely, despite the way he treated me.

Neither Mum nor Dad liked my wife because

she'd taken me away from the family home. Dad felt particularly betrayed by me. My wife and I ended up living in Plaistow, which was just far enough for my parents not to haunt us. I eventually had three children, two girls and a boy.

There was virtually no relationship between Dad and my kids after they were born. Dad was a bad communicator. Sometimes I wonder if the war affected people much more than we realise. I know he had a tough time back then. He did mention it a few times but he never even considered what Mum must have gone through in the bomb-ravaged East End.

Then I went out of my way to gain promotion above Dad. I became his manager, which meant he had to work for me. He didn't like that at all but he had no choice. However, I never once rubbed his nose in it, despite all that violence he had inflicted on me. After that, I became an accident investigations officer. Following the Moorgate tube disaster in 1974, I directed a ten-year programme to install extra safety measures. In 1987, I helped put King's Cross back to rights after more than 30 people lost their lives in that appalling disaster.

Yet I dealt with the horror of King's Cross a lot better than my relationship with Dad. A lot of us – the police and various Underground staff – would go and have a drink together afterwards and talk about it in the pub but none of us mentioned the full horrors at home. Back then, they offered no psychological support to Underground employees.

Anyway, me and my family moved to a big house as my job became more and more important. We had all the trappings: cars, swimming pool – you name it. I got divorced in 1991 after 18 years of marriage, although I can't blame the way I was treated by my father for that. I was working too hard. I got back from work one day and my wife was there with her friends, drinking by the pool. I asked her for a cup of tea and she said, 'Get it yerself.' I looked around and thought, I am paying for all this, and so I went out and had a couple of beers on my own. I realised then I had everything but nothing.

I suppose my father would have said the same to my mum but that was the trigger which changed my life. I ended up working a total of 31 years with the Underground and took early retirement in 1997, but it's only in the last few months that I've started dealing with what happened to me as a child. I'm now in a brilliant relationship and the future looks good. I'm living in a beautiful apartment on Spain's Costa del Sol, which must be the envy of many. Sometimes, I wonder if I chose to live abroad because those holidays with Mum and Dad were the only happy childhood memories I have.

Despite my newfound happiness, I still have one recurring nightmare. It has happened once a month for as long as I can remember. I'm in a car on my own and I'm backing into a space. I look into the rear-view mirror and there's nothing but a solid wall behind me. I hit the brakes but the car goes faster and faster. I hit the brakes again but I still keep going. Now I'm reversing at an incredibly high speed towards the wall, which is only a few feet away. I know I'm going to hit it. I'm still smashing my foot down on the brakes but it's not stopping. The wall is just inches away and then – I wake up.

Everyone in my family appears in my dreams except my dad. It's like I've blocked him out of my mind in just the same way I blocked his beatings out of my head throughout most of my childhood.

If my father were still alive today and he stepped out in front of my car on a road, I'd make sure I hit him. In fact, I'd hire a hit man to kill him if he suddenly turned up alive – or at least give him a really good hiding for what he did to me.

Yet I can also say, hand on heart, that I still love him.

7

Ginny

'WHY ME?' SHOULD be the title of my life story. It's the question I kept wanting to ask when I was a child but never had the courage to do so. I could have been a victim for the rest of my life but I won my battle, and now, although I still feel damaged, I've come out in one piece.

I was born in Cape Town, South Africa, and my parents got divorced when I was just six months old. Or at least that was the story I was told when I was growing up. But neither of them has ever properly come clean about why they split up. Recently, my mother wanted to pay for me to fly back to South Africa to find out more. But I'm still thinking over her offer. I have no memory of my parents as an actual couple, although they did remarry when I was two and then divorce again a year later.

I went to live with my father after the courts declared my mum unfit to bring me up. The first disturbing memory was when my dad started dating a 17-year-old girl. I was just five years old. I'd gone to my mum's for the weekend and she'd dropped me back at my dad's house on the Sunday night. I remember sitting on the porch of his huge mansion with my suitcase waiting for him and his teenage girlfriend to arrive back to let me in. It was pitch black and I was very scared sitting there all alone and it's made me terrified of the dark ever since. That evening was the first time I felt this overwhelming sense of not belonging.

Anyway, Dad finally showed up about two hours after I'd been dropped off by Mum. He laughed when I said I was scared waiting in the dark and his girlfriend just glared down at me sitting there on the step of the porch.

Life at my so-called proper home with Dad and his cute young lover soon became more difficult. At the beginning, she tried to win me over with gifts bought with Dad's money. That didn't help much. I just didn't want her to be close to my dad. I certainly didn't like the way she'd taken him away from my mother. I suppose we were competitors in a sense for

Dad's attention. She soon started referring to me as 'a little bitch'. Her favourite putdown was: 'You remind me of your mother and you're going to be the loser one day.'

There was a 17-year age gap between Dad and this girl. I later found out she'd given up a child for adoption at the age of 15. I suppose that's why when I was a teenager she used to beat me black and blue whenever I went out on dates, saying that I might get myself pregnant and ruin their good name. Now I look back on it, I realise she was trying to protect me, but she did it all wrong.

I suppose my father was quite a jealous man. My stepmother had a sexy body with big breasts, which made her quite attractive to men. But compared to my mum she was quite ugly. My mum was beautiful and had even been a model for ten years.

That young woman soon moved into my father's home. She was very fussy about my room being 100 per cent tidy and the first really traumatic experience occurred when she came into my room and found I'd put my shoes under my bed instead of in the cupboard. She exploded at me and made me take all the shoes out from under my bed and pile them in the middle of the floor. Then she made a grab for me. I knew she was going to hit me and tried to get away by jumping across the bed but then she tripped me up and I went flying. She then pulled the bed out and pushed my face down on it. Then she made me put my hands over the edge of the bed before slamming the bed against the wall which bent my wrists and felt agonising. I was soon in tears.

'You wait until your father gets home,' she shouted, as she pushed the bed backwards and forwards against that wall. 'You wait until your father gets home.'

Many other much worse things happened which I'll come to later, but there's one good memory that, thankfully, keeps coming back to me. I remember riding around on a little bicycle in the garden of my mum's tiny home, then running into the kitchen as my mum walked into another room. Then I jumped up and sat on the kitchen work-surface and grabbed this open tin of condensed milk and swallowed back the lot while her back was turned. It tasted so good. Some of it dribbled out of the corner of my mouth on to my chin and I remember the feeling when I caught those drops with my finger and licked it dry. That was a rarity in my childhood – a happy occasion. There weren't many of them and I think I must have been about five when it happened. But, every time the bad memories come flooding back, I switch back to that day in my mum's little home because it helps me realise that there were good things about my childhood.

The only time Dad ever hit me was when I was a bit older and we had an argument about staying out with a friend. The details are sketchy because I've blocked out most of it, but I remember he walked out of my bedroom after hitting me and then his girlfriend came in and tried to act all nice. I'm sure she was only doing that because she was so happy he'd beaten me. Dad never said sorry for hitting me that time. In fact, it was never spoken about ever again.

Dad and his young girlfriend – who was a nurse – got married when I was seven. I was the bridesmaid, which actually made me feel important for once. My new stepmother even bought me a Cindy doll with loads of clothes and told me that Cindy would look after me while they were away on honeymoon. But she got angry when I said I didn't believe her.

When I was nine, my half-sister was born. She meant the world to me because I was so desperate to have some company in that big rambling house with Dad and his young bride. But, looking back on it, that's when the beatings took a real turn for the worse.

We moved to a place called Springbok, a very Afrikaan area. We were known as 'the Engelsman' (Englishmen) because there were so many Boers in the area and Dad's family originally came from London. Dad then sent me to boarding school to get rid of me. I only went home once every four months.

It was a tough school, which was a big shock to me, although at least they cared about me there.

I once lost my temper at school when another girl insulted me about my real mother after she'd visited me. She called my mum a tart and taunted me about how young she dressed. After lights out in the dormitory, I took this wooden coat hanger, opened it up and got on top of one of the beds and beat this other girl so hard she almost passed out. Seeing what my temper could do was very scary for me and I've never lost it since.

The only thing I looked forward to at home was seeing my baby half-sister, although my stepmother told me never to push her pram in case I had an accident. One day, when there was no one in the garden and my baby sister was crying, I pushed the pram over a stone and it got stuck and the baby flew out and landed face first in the mud. My stepmother went ballistic. She came running out of the house, pulled hold of me and dragged me into the kitchen. She then grabbed a brush and started beating me on my bottom.

My father was in the house and must have known what was happening but did nothing to stop her laying into me. He later told me he was not prepared to risk upsetting his new young wife. Or as he put it: 'I'm not prepared to leave another marriage over you.' I didn't even know what he meant by that because no one had ever told me why he split from my mum.

One time, I answered my stepmother back and she dragged me into my bedroom with unbelievable strength. She took my hands and pinned me on the double bunk so I was hanging from the top bed. Then she grabbed me by the neck while I was dangling in the air and started smashing my face into the side of the bed. This went on for at least five minutes until my face started to turn blue.

This time my father actually stepped in to stop it. I think he was worried she might kill me. 'What the hell are you doing?' he asked her.

She then dropped me on to the floor like a sack of potatoes before spitting down at me that I was 'a little bitch' and storming out of the room. That weekend, I went to visit my mum and she noticed the marks on my neck and face but she didn't confront my father about what had happened because she was afraid of them both. After another later attack, Mum actually took photographs of my injuries and went to a lawyer to try to get custody of me but the fees were more than she could afford so she gave up.

In public, my stepmother seemed the model parent. She was the caring, sharing nurse who attended to the sick at the local hospital. She went to church every Sunday and always did everything right.

She never even swore. But at home she'd unleash her violent temper on her step-daughter. Her latest insult was to call me a slut all the time. Later, I concluded that Dad must have told her my mum was having an affair with one of his friends and that's why she called me that.

I stayed in boarding school for two years. Then we moved to a town near Johannesburg, because of my dad's job as a company manager. I hated being back at home full time.

My stepmother hit me at least three times a week from then on. She bashed me so many times I can't remember one beating from another. I don't honestly know if I even went to hospital. Everything back then is now just a blur.

I do recall one time she hit me so badly that clots of blood shot out of my nostrils. I remember looking down at the palm of my hand and it was covered in these blobs of blood. My father knew what his wife was doing to me but did little to stop it. Sometimes, it felt as if she had some magical hold over him.

One time, my stepmother attacked me in front of my half-sister and she helped pull her off me. My stepmother still tried to hit me. But she never touched her own child. I had to take the brunt of all her frustrations and anger because I dared to answer her back.

I'd become the black sheep of the family. I was given this bedroom well away from everyone else on the other side of our five garages. Even when I was only about nine, I was living a strangely isolated life. It was my stepmother who'd decided where my bedroom should be. Draw your own conclusions from that.

Most days, my father would send me on what he pleasantly called 'shit duty' to pick up all the dog poo in our huge garden. I also had to mow the lawn. Afterwards, I'd sit on the grass at the end of the garden for hours, well away from prying eyes. Then I'd pluck these enormous sharp thorns from a booringbos (thorn tree) and push them into my knuckles until I bled to take away the hurt I was feeling inside. I thought of nothing. I don't know why I did it. The pain was extreme but it stopped me flipping out with anyone and no one even noticed the wounds on my hands.

I went to eight schools as a child. I had few true friends. I tried to be trusting but I always kept a barrier up. I knew everyone but was close to virtually no one. At school, I was academically useless but good at gymnastics, tennis and athletics and thrived on competitiveness. It all helped me stay out of the house longer so I could avoid those awful clashes with my stepmother.

One of my few real friends lived five doors up and her family were very easygoing. Their home became my little haven. They knew I was being beaten. My stepmother never liked them and even tried to stop me going there. Often I'd go straight there from school. My stepmother would then phone the house and order them to send me back home.

I was never allowed to have anyone to stay in our house. But my stepmother made a big deal over birthdays and would bake a cake and invite her friends around for my birthday. She always made sure they were the trendiest people in the community. She liked keeping up with the Joneses. The fact it was actually my birthday became an irrelevance. Dad was always out of the house working but then I don't blame him for wanting to get away from her.

My stepmother used to collect teaspoons and I painted this massive African map and she used to pin the spoons wherever she'd travelled. She also adored porcelain dolls. My father worked his butt off to keep her. We moved constantly because she wanted a better house. One time, he paid for a factory kiln so she could make pottery. Then she wanted to own an old people's home and they converted a mansion but she soon got bored and Dad eventually sold it at a massive loss.

The feeling of exclusion from my own family was

further fuelled by the fact there were no photos of me on the mantelpiece alongside my half-sister. Also, my father and stepmother never came to see me in sporting events at school. I remember getting medals for gymnastics and a major tennis trophy and no one from my family was there to see me on my big day.

In the middle of all this violence and unhappiness, my stepmother's 25-year-old brother took pity on me and showed me a lot of care and attention. He knew what was going on and was very understanding and provided a wonderful shoulder to cry on. Earlier, he'd even bought me my first tennis racket and encouraged me to play. He really spoiled me and became my rock of stability at the time. I was 12 years old and feeling incredibly lonely and isolated in Dad's huge house, which was dominated by this woman who seemed intent on beating me to death.

I suppose you'd call him my step-uncle. Anyway, and this is where the hard bit comes in, he started a full sexual relationship with me. It lasted until my first boyfriend when I was 15. Back at the time, I really thought we were in love. He used to say he loved me and would take me to his place at weekends. I actually thought at one stage that we'd eventually get married.

He lived about an hour away on a massive, isolated chicken farm where he was the manager. Obviously, neither my father or stepmother suspected anything.

As far as they were concerned, he was being a good, responsible uncle and he was taking troublesome me off their hands.

Anyway, we would have really intimate barbecues together at his home, put the music on and dance together and then go to bed. He became my companion, lover, confidante. He told me to keep it all a secret and that it was all just between us. It was something special and he promised it would always stay that way.

Eventually, I met a boy of my own age and fell in love with him. It was only then that I realised the situation with my stepmother's brother was completely wrong. The new boyfriend was a proper relationship and I felt what you were supposed to feel when you were in love.

A couple of years later, many family members – including my step-uncle – were at my father's house and he'd had a drink and we were sitting up talking. I guess I was about 16. By then I was sleeping in an outside room on the other side of the garages, well away from everyone else.

I'd just started work – it's against the law in South Africa to leave school before you're 18 but I'd left early.

Anyway, my step-uncle tried to kiss me in the hallway away from everyone else. I pushed him away but he carried on until I said to him, 'I'm gonna call my father unless you stop it. Enough is enough.' Then he stopped. I've never seen him since.

My father's views on romance were pretty unpleasant. When I was 16, he issued me with the following four rules and said I had to follow them if I wanted to live in his house:

1. Don't ever date a limey (Englishman).
2. Don't ever date someone with long hair and tattoos and piercings.
3. Don't ever date a black man.
4. Don't ever date a Jew.

I broke every rule except for the tattoos. I was definitely not a racist like Dad.

Back then, I suffered from really heavy period pains, as well as being deeply unhappy about my life. My stepmother recommended a gynaecologist to me. He wanted to know if I was sexually active and it was very difficult because my first sexual relationship had been with her brother when I was 12. Obviously, he could see I was no longer a virgin but I refused to tell him about my sex life and especially my step-uncle. When I got home that day, my stepmother said to me, 'What did you say to the gynaecologist?'

'I'm not telling you,' I said. 'It's none of your

business. I wouldn't even tell my mother so why should I tell you?'

'I want to know,' she snapped back.

Then she shouted at me to get out and followed me down the stairs towards my room at the other side of the house. She kept saying, 'You will, you little bitch. You will tell me or you will tell your father.'

Then she grabbed me by my hair and started yanking me back up the stairs. Then she pushed me and I almost fell down the stairs.

'Right, you're out!' she yelled. 'You get out tonight!'

That night, I sat with my baby sister's nanny Rula in her outhouse in the grounds of our house. We had a cigarette and a drink together and afterwards I jumped the fence at the back of our huge garden and ran five blocks down the road to the place where I worked.

I knocked next door at the home of a woman who was the receptionist and her parents let me stay the night. They could see I was in a state. Later, I heard that my stepmother had admitted to my father what had happened and he then got in his car and drove all night looking for me without success.

I didn't return home for two months. Then, in the middle of all this, I tried to commit suicide. I was in the staff room and grabbed a cutthroat razor and tried to cut myself. It was a cry for help. One of my workmates walked in and caught me doing it. They sent me home and that was the first time, my dad and real mother ever sat down together in a room and tried to sort out their relationship.

My dad agreed that it was best I didn't come home and he would pay the extra amount of money so I could live somewhere else. I was only being paid 185 rand a month and the rent on a flat was 220.

I didn't tell anyone what happened with my step-uncle until a few years ago when I was staying with my family back in South Africa and it all came out. My stepmother and I had another row as usual. She told me I didn't know what having a hard life was all about and my boyfriend Jack looked at me and said, 'Now is the time to tell them.' I couldn't come out with it so he shouted out at them, 'Your brother sexually molested Ginny,' and that was it.

My stepmother jumped over the kitchen counter, went for me in front of my boyfriend's parents and then decked my boyfriend. She was screaming, 'You're a liar and a bloody whore!' and then charged out of the door.

My father looked at me and said, 'What have you done?'

'It's the truth, Dad,' I replied.

'Then there must be some truth in it,' he conceded guardedly.

For the first time in his life, he seemed to be

backing me up. It was 11pm. At 12.30am, my half-sister phoned me to say my stepmother had still not come home. She eventually arrived home covered in cuts and bruises. She was very drunk and had fallen into some bushes.

My dad phoned me at 2.30 that same morning and said he wanted me to take a lie-detector test later that day at 11am.

I said, 'Fine, but after I've taken it I will denounce you as my father.'

I was insulted that he would even consider getting me to take a lie-detector test. That meant he didn't trust me, his own daughter.

Then Dad phoned me at 10.30 that morning to say he had confronted my step-uncle who'd denied it. Then my step-uncle phoned just before the lie-detector test was due to go ahead and said he'd just told my father we'd slept together by mutual consent, and he thought it was best we swept it all under the carpet and got on with our lives. I walked into Dad's office later that day after he'd refused to speak to me again on the phone. I said, 'If you're not going to phone me, then I'm here to say goodbye.'

That was 16 December 2000. We called off Christmas that year and I have not spoken to my father since. When I went into therapy, I was asked to give an honest opinion of my parents and I said,

'My mum was incredibly glamorous looking which I found intimidating. My father was a coward and my stepmother went out of her way to earn the name "bitch".'

That's all I can say about them but in some weird way I still love my mum and dad.

I have many people who come into my hairdressing salon with whom I can empathise. I think I have chosen this career because there is a lot of psychology in hairdressing. One girl came into my salon and said she hated herself, her family and everything she stood for. She didn't want to live any more. So I turned to her and said, 'If you hate yourself so much, why do you come in here and have your hair done?' I never heard from her again. It didn't make sense. Why be here spending money if you don't love yourself? I don't know if that was the right or wrong answer but it summed up her situation.

My dad had a stroke a few months ago. He is weak but the doctors say he'll live. I would like to sit down and write him a long letter. I have constant conversations with myself about the things I want to say to my parents but I've never got round to it. I love them, but my father is a coward. I was a child put in a situation I should never have been put into. He wasn't grown up about it. He should have taken my side. He helped create me and he should have helped protect me. I should have been his number-one priority.

I was always scared that I would treat my kids the way I was treated. I would have loved to be a mother but doctors told me recently I could never have any children of my own, so I'll never know the real answer. I suspect those beatings by my stepmother may be responsible.

The truth is I have never trusted a woman in my life as a result of what happened to me. I would trust a man more and that is scary because so many of the men in my life have taken full advantage of me.

But now I've found someone I truly believe I am going to stay with for the rest of my life. We're building our dream home in the countryside. I've got a successful hairdressing business and I've left all that brutality far behind. But there's not a day that goes by when I don't think about my childhood.

8

Jimmy

MY STEPDAD DENNIS came on the scene when I was about 11 years old and that's when my whole life turned upside down. Up until then, we'd been a relatively tight, happy family unit, even after the old man did a runner when I was eight. There was me, my brother Mickey and Mum in a tidy little two-bed semi-detached house in Wanstead, east London.

My dad was well upset when Dennis appeared because he was one of his old school mates. As a result, Dennis was always tense when Dad turned up to see us. But, when I look back on it, Dennis was tense all the time. He was short and stocky with dark hair and a scar down the side of his left cheek and he was always ducking and diving. I reckon that's why he flew off the handle so easily. He had too much on his mind. He boasted about meeting some well-known faces when he did time inside, and he always seemed to be watching his back, as if other villains were after him.

It took a couple of years before I realised that Dennis was knocking my mum around. Sometimes, I'd come home from school and notice the atmosphere between them was a bit tense, but it never seemed that serious. Then he started snapping at me, especially at mealtimes. Sometimes, I'd get a slap round the head for my troubles. Then one day he dragged me out back and gave me a hiding for nicking a tin of his precious Special Brew. I soon grew to hate him with a vengeance.

By the time I reached 13, I was going out of my way to avoid Dennis. When he walked in a room, I walked out. When he talked to me – which was rare – I gave him a short, sharp answer. By now, I'd been on the receiving end a good few times and I was well aware of his bullying tactics. I'd also started to notice the cuts and bruises on Mum's arms and legs. She'd brush them off by saying she'd banged the corner of a table or whatever. But now I was on the lookout for Dennis. I knew there were problems and I suspected that he'd been whacking Mum. So I suppose it was kind of inevitable when me and my older brother Mickey walked in from football practice and opened the back door into the kitchen to find Dennis lashing out at my tiny little mum with both fists.

Mum was cowering beneath him. I exploded. We both tried to drag Dennis off her. But then he got me by the throat and started squeezing tight. Mickey smashed him over the head with a vase and he finally let go and stormed out of the house. It was all over in less than a couple of minutes but that didn't make it any easier to deal with.

'What you doin' with that arsehole, Mum?' I asked her after the dust had settled.

She just shrugged her shoulders and I knew what that meant – she'd give Dennis the benefit of the doubt yet again. Mum had always brought us up to respect people's feelings. 'If they don't bother you,' she'd say, 'you leave them well alone.' As a result, me and my brothers were never involved in any fights at school or stuff like that. But, back at home, we were being dragged into a conflict that seemed destined to end in bloodshed.

We tolerated Dennis in the house because Mum seemed to still adore him, although it was difficult to understand why. Looking back on it, I reckon she was terrified of being on her own again and that's why she put up with him.

Over the following year, I threw myself into

boxing, convinced that it held the key to my future. I was doing well in the ring and could pack a mean punch. The trainers at the local Boys Club all reckoned I'd go far and the idea of using my fists to fight my way out of poverty really appealed to me.

Even then, I felt a deep responsibility towards my family. I wanted to do good by them. I wanted them to be proud of me. I also wanted to be strong and fit enough to give Dennis the thrashing he deserved if I ever caught him hurting Mum again.

It was a bitterly cold winter's day and the icy wind was biting into my cheeks as I struggled along the street towards my family home after yet another waste-of-time day at school. I was 14 years old and desperate to escape into the real world, earn a living and get on with my life.

As I ran up the dog-shit-infested path to our house, I heard screaming and shouting – a sound that had so often filled my childhood. Mum was yelling about something or other with Dennis. She was really giving him a hard time. Probably about his bad temper again or maybe he'd gone and disappeared for a few days, as he sometimes did when he was up to no good.

I stopped at the entrance to our front door and took a deep breath. Did I really want to walk into yet another row after the sort of day I'd just had at school? I was tempted to turn round and head off for the local park and my little hideaway amongst the trees and bushes where me and my mates would escape the pressures and unhappiness of our homes. But that day it was too bloody cold so I steeled myself for some verbal abuse and pulled out my doorkey.

My hand was shaking like a leaf. Was it the cold or the fear that I was about to walk into a war zone? After a couple of seconds, I managed to steady my hand enough to slide the key into the Yale lock. Just then a male voice screamed, 'You fuckin' bitch! Don't you ever fuckin' talk to me like that!'

Then I heard the unmistakable thud of a fist connecting with flesh. That snivelling little piece of shit of a stepdad was at it again. Mum started crying and screaming all at the same time. It was a horrible, disturbing blend of noises.

'You want some more? You fuckin' want some more?' he yelled.

'I hate you! I hate you! I hate you!' came Mum's reply.

I rushed up the hallway into the kitchen. Mum's face was all blown up like a balloon and I immediately knew what he'd done to her, even though she was turning away to try and stop me seeing the state of her face. Dennis looked down at the floor in order to avoid my gaze.

My eyes narrowed to try to stop the tears of anger welling up. Without saying another word, I ran straight at Dennis, whacked him in the face and then followed up with a flurry of right hooks. He cowered down to try to stop the punches connecting but he was no match for the sheer force of my anger.

The sound of my fists pounding into his body permeated the kitchen. It started something like this: tap... tap... with my left fist. As I pushed my arms away from my body, my bastard stepdad took a swing at me but he missed because I ducked too fast for him.

Then I popped a vicious right into his battered, leathery old face. It felt like a hard shot and he quivered after I connected. That's when I really steamed into him: left, left... and then right... WHACK! Left, left... right... WHACK! Left, left... right... WHACK! Air wheezed out of him with every punch.

Mum looked on, aware that the shots I was targeting on her partner were going to stop him ever hurting her again. We both knew it was time to say goodbye to this arsehole for good.

I finally stepped back as he crumpled to the floor. Then he looked up at me with an expression of sheer hatred on his face. He looked set on coming at me again.

'Don't move!' I screamed at him.

But he ignored me and continued getting up from the floor.

'I said, "Don't fuckin' move!"'

But he wasn't listening and began veering in my direction. I grabbed a carving fork off the sideboard and faced him with it clutched in my left hand. He got even closer.

'Stay away!' I screamed.

'Fuck off!' he spat, just managing to get the words out from his blood-filled mouth.

Then he turned in the direction of Mum. The mere notion that he might be about to start hurting her again left me with no choice but to stick the fork right in the side of his stomach. I heard the hiss of escaping air as it pierced through flesh and fat. I didn't mean to do it. It was just a defensive reaction. I immediately pulled the fork out with all my strength and found myself staring down at the bloody piece of kitchen cutlery in the palm of my hand.

Moments later, he doubled up in agony and fell on all fours on to the floor. I looked down at him, still gripping the fork in my right hand. Then he began crawling towards the door. I stared at him for a few more seconds while he slithered into the hallway. Then I stepped forward and kicked him hard as he stumbled down the steps.

I hoped we'd never see him again.

Less than an hour later, the coppers came knocking at our front door and said Dennis had lodged a complaint against me and Mickey, alleging we'd tried to kill him. Can you believe it? That slimy bastard had not only taken a pop at my poor little, defenceless mum but he'd gone and grassed me up to the law and tried to make out Mickey was involved as well. The police wanted to take me and Mickey down to the nick, so I put my hand up and admitted I'd done the fighting so they wouldn't take Mickey away.

That night I was locked in a cell at the local police station. Dennis pressed for me to be charged with Grievous Bodily Harm (GBH). He must have really hated me. I was shit scared and close to tears when they locked the door of that cell. I was suddenly all alone. I threw myself on to the half-inch-thick mattress against the wall and cried myself to sleep that night, not because I was afraid of being in custody but because I couldn't understand how I'd allowed things to get so out of hand. I was also angry with Mum for letting Dennis into her life in the first place, although his violence could never be put down to her.

Next morning, they hauled me out of the cell and I gave a statement admitting what had happened. If I hadn't stuck that fork in him, then maybe I wouldn't have been so harshly treated. One of the coppers said that using a so-called 'weapon' turned it from a common assault charge to GBH.

I've got to say here and now the Old Bill were fairly decent to me. They only cuffed me when they had to and they didn't rough me up at all. Round where I lived you expected a few problems down the local nick, but they were as good as gold. I think they felt sorry for me because Dennis was so clearly a toe-rag. One of the coppers pulled me aside and said he thought it was a disgrace that a big fella like Dennis could press charges against a 14-year-old kid. He reckoned I'd severely damaged Dennis's pride more than anything else and that fork had only caused a wound which would heal in a few weeks.

I admitted the GBH charge so they held the trial within a couple of days of my arrest. As I had no previous record, I thought I'd get off with a community service order. I was – and still am – a shy sort of bloke, so all these people staring at me in court made me shrink even more into myself. I even caught a glimpse of that bastard Dennis smirking at me from across the courtroom. I answered all the questions with a short 'yes' or 'no' and I could tell that was irritating court officials. Then there was Mum in the public gallery close to tears. This was her baby in the dock because he'd defended her against the man she now hated more than anyone else in the world.

The magistrate gave me three months' youth detention. My legs wobbled for a few seconds after he said it. I couldn't quite believe my ears. Then Mum stood up and shouted at Dennis, 'He's the one you should be locking up.' Earlier, she'd even tried to press counter charges but the police told her not to bother.

I was taken away in cuffs. I was about to serve a stretch inside for defending my tiny, fragile mum against a 14-stone bully who'd tried to smash her – and me – to a pulp once too often. Something wasn't right, but I was too young and too scared to say anything. My head bowed and I just took the punishment. I was numbed and resigned to what had happened. I didn't fight. I didn't try to have a bundle with the guards. I just went quietly.

Minutes later, I was pushed into the back of a dark-blue Transit van with blacked-out windows and headed off to Her Majesty's Borstal, in Rochester, Kent, which was – I would soon discover – one of the worst youth detention centres in the whole of Britain. The screws picked up three other kids on the way there. Two of them were crying throughout the journey, which didn't make things any easier. Meanwhile, I sat in the back chained up like a rabid dog, trying not to look too worried. But, beneath the brave exterior, I was in tatters. I felt broken and wasted. And I wondered if I'd ever get my life on track again.

I eventually got out of Borstal and none of us – including Mum – ever saw that evil bastard Dennis again. Now I'm married to a wonderful girl with two beautiful daughters and life is sweet. Today, I thank my lucky stars that I didn't take a permanent wrong turning all those years ago when I was sent to Borstal just for defending my mother against a man who'd physically abused us after he'd moved into our home.

I think I've proved that it doesn't matter how much damage you suffer as a child, there's always a way out of that cycle of violence. I hope my story is an inspiration to people but I would say here and now that you should never take the retribution route. I don't regret what I did to my stepfather but it so nearly cost me my entire life. I would say to anyone in a similar situation, 'Get away from the bad people. Don't try and take them on.' You have to cut them out like a dose of cancer before they kill you either emotionally or physically.

9

Jenny

MY LIFE CHANGED forever when I was eight years old and returned home from a weekend away at the seaside with my father Peter and my uncle Derek. We'd stayed at the White Cliffs Hotel in Dover, and I'd had a brilliant time being Daddy's little girl at the centre of everyone's attention. I was allowed to eat with the grown-ups, stay up late and even engaged in some very adult conversations. I remember feeling on top of the world when I got home.

But, after my return home, my mother Susan behaved differently towards me. She seemed angry and dismissive and later all this would spill out into pure venom.

Anyway, the day we got home from that trip, Mummy did a huge family Sunday lunch at the hotel in Brighton that my father managed and which was our home. Being in charge of a hotel is like being on the stage every night and it was very difficult for him to switch off sometimes.

My sister and three brothers were at the lunch and I remember wondering why Mummy had put on such a huge bash when we'd only been away one night. But then, as we sat down for the lunch, I looked across at my mother and there was this horrible expression on her face. It was as if she was thinking, You tart, although I didn't work that out until much later. At the lunch that day, my mother tried everything to make my father happy, serving him all his food, pouring his wine and looking adoringly in his direction virtually every second of the day. If only I had understood why.

Even though I was only eight years old, I knew I'd done something wrong in her eyes. I just wasn't sure what it was. I remember feeling guilty because Mummy was so clearly cross with me. It bothered me so much but, as I've said, I was too young to work it out back then.

My relationship with my father had always been close. Way before we ever went away to Dover that time, I used to spend many lovely Saturday afternoons at home, sitting on Daddy's knee on his chunky leather Parker Knoll chair. I'd kiss and cuddle him and play with his ear, while Mummy sat staring in irritation across the room from us. Poor Mummy. She seemed so unhappy.

I remember Daddy picking me up and swinging me around which he would never do to my sister and brothers. I suppose all that loving care and attention turned me into what they call these days a really touchy-feely child. I wanted to be with my daddy all the time. Mummy didn't seem so keen on me but there wasn't much I could do about that.

But, not long after I got back from that night away with my father and uncle, my parents started fighting and I soon retreated into my own private little world. I was already by nature what you'd call 'a carer'. I wanted everyone around me to be happy. I didn't like hearing Mummy and Daddy arguing late into the night. I'd try to block it out by pulling the pillow over my head but I still kept listening to them in case it gave me any clues as to the future. I felt incredibly insecure at the very thought of my father not being around. And, in the daytime, my mother treated me more and more like a love rival than a daughter, convinced (as I was to later discover) that something had happened between me and Daddy when we went to Dover for that night away with my uncle.

Mummy and I had a lot of fights, although at first most of them were only really shouting matches. She never mentioned that she thought Daddy had done something to me. All I could feel was an undercurrent of hatred radiating from her. I was always the one she picked on. I could never do anything right. Meanwhile, my siblings never got into any trouble.

My 12-year-old brother David was even more upset than I was by my parents' constant bickering. I'd often catch him swigging from his own bottle of vodka, which he kept hidden behind the sofa in the drawing room when he watched television. David was treated strangely by my parents. He was a boarder at a nearby public school, even though we lived so close to the school we could see him when he was out in the playing fields. That must have been so difficult for David because he was always so desperate to come home.

One night, when Mummy and Daddy were rowing, I remember seeing David crying in his bed. Even though I was only eight years old I could see he needed comforting, so I tried to cheer him up by telling him some funny stories and giving him a cuddle in bed as our parents continued slagging each other off downstairs. I recall he was shaking at one stage and sobbed on my shoulder for ages. I tried so hard to make him feel better. I felt so sorry for David and I desperately wanted him to cheer up. Even back then, I was, as I've already said, the ultimate carer.

In a proper, secure family unit, my brother's unhappy behaviour would never have been left to me to sort out. My mother should have been aware that her eight-year-old daughter was having to play mummy to her oldest son. But neither of my parents noticed any of it because they were so wrapped up in their own problems.

As far as I was concerned, David needed me and I had to make him feel better. My father never got on well with David and maybe it was that sense of rejection which made him so desperately unhappy. Daddy had been to Winchester College public school and then gone to Cambridge. He was an Olympic swimmer who almost won a bronze medal. He wanted my brother to follow in his footsteps and was so disappointed in him. It must have put David under immense pressure.

The atmosphere in the house continued to get worse and worse. And, looking back on it, I remained the odd one out. Mummy even made me sleep in a bedroom on my own while my sister and baby brothers slept in another bedroom. She never explained why and I never asked. I was on my own and that made me feel even more vulnerable.

Then the atmosphere in our home took a turn for the worse. By now, my parents were sleeping in separate bedrooms and we all knew that the end of their marriage was in sight. One night, I walked into Mummy's bedroom to say goodnight and found her unconscious with an empty bottle of pills on the floor. I was too young to know exactly what this meant, but I knew Mummy was sick. Her body seemed to be twitching and rising in spasms off the floor. It was quite surreal to watch and I'll never forget it as long as I live. My sister and brothers were asleep so I knocked on Daddy's door and said, 'Daddy, Daddy, I think you should call the ambulance because Mummy's ill.' The last I saw of her was as she was stretchered out of the flat.

Back then, mothers of five children who tried to commit suicide didn't get much sympathy from the doctors and nurses. If only they'd known why she'd made such a desperate plea for help. Later, I convinced myself it was what had happened on that night away with my father and uncle which prompted Mummy's attempt on her own life.

For two days, none of us even knew if Mummy was alive or dead. Then my father took us to see her. He gave us each a bunch of flowers to take in to Mummy and I remember being angry because really it was all his fault she had tried to kill herself. If only he would give her more attention and forget about me, I used to think to myself.

Virtually everything that happened back then was

connected to my mother and father fighting in front of us. I remember one night, when we were living in another hotel and our accommodation consisted of a flat in the basement, and it sticks in my mind because Daddy was carrying Mummy in his arms and laughing and joking and I was thinking, Oh good, they're having a nice evening. And then out of the blue Mummy said to Daddy, 'Why are you fucking that bitch?' The atmosphere changed in a split second and they stared arguing. I thought, Why are you going on at him again? Go to bed. Be happy. OK, so he might have been having an affair with another woman, but I was the sort of character even back then who always wanted a peaceful solution to all problems.

Well, Daddy was a big man and he really lost it that evening. He laid into Mummy with his fists. I heard most of it from my bedroom, which was right next door to where they were. I cried myself to sleep that night.

Next morning, I thought my mother had a blood disorder because she had so many bruises on her arms and legs. Later, I'd often ask her about a particular bruise and she'd say, 'If I hit myself on a table, it comes up. I must ask the doctor what I can take to stop it.'

Eventually and, I suppose, inevitably, the stress got to my darling daddy and he began hitting me as well.

He'd kick me if I didn't shut the door when I left the drawing room where he'd often sit alone drinking malt whisky. I remember getting booted from one end of the house to the other by him on numerous other occasions. Often, he'd whack me on the bottom if I tried to get away from him. I remember Mummy coming out of her bedroom as he was hitting me and saying, 'Don't you dare touch my daughter!'

I was scared of Dad. But that was the norm back then. Mind you, when I listen to other people's childhoods, they all sound much better than mine. I was especially hurt because I thought I was his special little girl. He'd told me as much when we'd been away that time in Dover with Uncle Derek when I slept in their room because I was scared to be on my own.

Whenever Mummy and Daddy got into a really nasty physical fight, I'd think it was all my fault. He'd punch and slap her and then they'd notice me and simply move to another room to continue their fight. Most of this violence must have been born out of his frustration because he no longer wanted to be with us.

Daddy was using violence to punish us for his own unhappiness. Yet, throughout all this, Mummy remained completely and utterly in love with my father. Mummy still talks about him to this day as her husband, even though she's been married to another man for almost 20 years. But then

Mummy's never been very good at moving on. I think that's why she made me feel so bad about going away with him and my uncle that night. It seemed to burn a hole in her heart.

By this time, I was well aware of Mummy's attitude towards me and her suspicions that something happened when I was with Daddy in that hotel but it did nothing to water down my love for Daddy. I still felt this closeness to him, which, in some twisted way, had been fuelled by how we had shared that hotel bedroom a couple of years earlier.

I was devastated when my parents split up when I was ten years old but at least all the beatings immediately stopped. I missed my father so much I wrote to him every week for a year saying I didn't want to be with my mother. I adored him so much despite the violence and her overwhelming suspicion that he'd done something to me when we were in that hotel. I believed I would be much happier in his company but, in those days, the mother always got custody. A year after they parted, my father let it slip to my mother that I'd sent him all those letters and she called me a 'fucking little bitch'.

Whenever I told Mummy I didn't want to be with her, we'd start behaving like two women fighting for the affections of the same man. She'd tell me I couldn't go with him. That it wasn't healthy for me.

That word 'healthy' came back to haunt me in later life because it definitely wasn't very healthy for a little girl to share a hotel room with two men.

Shortly after my parents finally split up, I went to stay with friends rather than live with my mother. Even at ten years old, I knew how to deal with what had happened between my parents, although I still desperately wanted it all to be back to the way it was.

Here I was, the ultimate provider even at that young age. I was the one who helped everyone. I said enough is enough. Years later – long after their divorce – I spoke to Mummy about Daddy's violence towards us and pointed out, 'I had a pretty disastrous childhood.'

Mummy went ballistic: 'What d'you mean? I did my best for you.'

'I'm really sorry, Mum – I didn't mean it.' I backed down completely but that's typical of the way I've always led my life. Instead of going for her and wondering why she wasn't there when I was an eight-year-old playing mother to my 12-year-old brother, I didn't confront her. But every time I got a hint of her disapproval, I knew it was connected to what happened in that hotel room I'd shared with Daddy and Uncle Derek.

It wasn't until I was 30 years old that I actually confronted Mummy about the night in the hotel room. I think I wanted to shock her so I blurted out that my father had abused me. She hit the roof, screaming and shouting at me in the middle of the road. 'You fucking bitch. You're telling me your father abused you? You're saying that? How dare you?'

She'd been the one who'd made me believe he'd hurt me, but she couldn't stand to hear that it might have happened. It multiplied her feelings of jealousy, even all those years later. My father didn't want to touch her but he'd touched me. It tortured her to even think about it. Of course, I felt bad but she'd been so horrible to me for so long that I was glad she was upset.

My mother's reaction was so extreme that I didn't tell anyone else what had happened with Daddy. I wasn't close to him any more so we never mentioned that night in the hotel and, in a strange way, I still needed his approval for certain aspects of my life.

When I reached 35 years old, my second marriage began dissolving into chaos and I was offered Prozac, which I refused because my husband was already on it. So I opted for clinical help instead and went to a therapist. I just shrugged my shoulders and told the therapist how my father had abused me. He seemed shocked that I was being so laid back about it. As far as I was concerned, I needed to move on.

Poor Daddy heard I was seeing a shrink. He never even dared phone me up for a chat because he was afraid I might confront him. He knew my head was a bit screwed up, so he was always very sensitive towards me. But now he was the one doing the suffering. I thought it was the least he deserved for taking advantage of me all those years earlier.

Then, during my next session with the therapist, something weird happened. Like a bolt out of nowhere, this lightbulb went off in my head and I realised Daddy had never laid a finger on me. This therapist had made me look back at my childhood in real detail and I realised there was nothing there. The therapist said I had worked very hard and that I was not the person I had at first seemed to be. I'd always used my sexuality as a façade and he said when he first met me he thought that was what I was, just a shallow person prepared to use sex to my own advantage. But he said that, having got to know me, he now realised I was a good person, and hearing that from a stranger made me realise for the first time in my life I was not to blame. It's very odd but the moment that feeling came over me I knew that my father had done nothing inappropriate towards me apart from being a loving, caring parent. It seems so ridiculous that my mother could become so eaten up with jealousy that she'd subconsciously convinced me that Daddy had hurt me.

Knowing that my father hadn't done anything to

me was such a relief. It changed my life around. I became like a different person. It's just so strange the way it came to me and it certainly makes me wonder about so many of these cases involving delayed memory syndrome.

I was so happy. I don't blame anyone apart from my mother. She was obsessed with getting my father's attention, not me. I've never spoken to my mother about it because I still believe she thinks something did occur, even though she didn't want to hear it when I told her.

When he was dying from cancer shortly afterwards, I pleaded for his forgiveness as he lay on his deathbed. He was pumped up with morphine as I held his hand and said, 'Dad, I know you didn't hurt me. I'm so sorry.'

I don't know if he heard me but I hope and pray he did.

Now I'm 42 years old and I've finally found true happiness with a man I wish I'd met 20 years ago because then I would have avoided two unhappy marriages. He listens to me and understands what I've been through and how it has affected my character. We live a pleasant, gentle life close to the sea but away from all the pain and anguish I put my father through, even though my partner keeps telling me none of it was my fault.

10

Marie

MY NAME IS Marie and I was born in 1958 in Budapest, Hungary, just after the Soviets invaded to prevent an anti-Communist uprising – a war that cost my grandfather his valuable property empire. My family were originally Turks who had moved to Hungary, and hundreds of years ago, when Hungary was part of the Turkish empire, my family thrived.

My grandfather was so devastated by the Soviet invasion in 1956 that he turned to drink and eventually became a chronic alcoholic, which caused a lot of the abuse I suffered as a child. My grandmother came from a very poor farming family and married well above her class. During World War II, my grandfather was made to serve in the German army and had to walk back to Hungary after the

Nazis were defeated. He'd lost everything, but then he moved to Budapest where he started buying properties once more. Then the 1956 revolution came and he lost it all again. My family were part of the political counter-revolution at that time.

My grandfather became a postman after losing everything. He and my grandmother took in my parents and me because few people could afford their own houses back then. My father had ended up working for the Communist party, although he was really more of an artistic dreamer than a political hardliner, and my parents worked virtually around the clock at each of their jobs, so mainly it was my grandmother who brought me up.

When I was three years old, my grandmother accidentally burned my bottom by sitting me on the cooker. My mother thought this was hilariously funny and even took me into her office, where she pulled down my pants and showed everyone how burned my bottom was. I don't know why she did it. It was very embarrassing and it is something I've never forgotten.

The first actual violence I can remember as a child was when I saw my drunken grandfather chasing my grandmother across the garden with a knife. At first, I thought they were playing a silly game. Then I heard my grandmother scream when he lunged at her and

I realised this was far from funny. Luckily, my grandmother wasn't injured. My grandfather had also been a very abusive father and beaten my mother and her sister with a bat. But, by the time I came on the scene, he'd switched his hatred towards my grandmother. But I was too young back then to know why he did it.

I was left on my own much of the time and soon created my own little world that kept me apart from the normal everyday problems. As a result, I grew up much more quickly than most kids did. From an early age, no one really disciplined me at all. The streets of Budapest were considered safe so we played outside virtually all day.

I remember I hated it when my mother first took me to kindergarten. I was four at the time and I hung on to the door for dear life because I didn't want to go in. In the end, I had to be dragged kicking and screaming into school. No one – including my mother – bothered to wonder why I was so against going to school. I hated the food. I hated the teachers and, above all, I hated my classmates. I just wanted to return to my own little world at home.

That afternoon, I waited and waited for my mother to turn up to collect me from kindergarten but she didn't turn up. I cried my eyes out. It wasn't until seven in the evening that she finally appeared and offered no excuse except to say she had been at work. That was always my mother's answer to everything. Work. I'd sat there all afternoon worrying and she didn't even say sorry.

I continued not wanting to go to kindergarten and soon my mother was beating me regularly to make me go. She'd drag me out of the house by my hair sometimes, not caring who might be witnessing this violence. The blows would rain down on my head and she'd scream at me that I had to go to school otherwise she couldn't go to work and then we'd have no money and die of starvation. Back at home, my grandmother cooked repulsive reheated old food most evenings, so I rarely ate a proper meal. No wonder I needed my secret world.

From the age of five, I walked to and from school alone. I accepted school more once I was allowed that important measure of independence. I saw all sorts of things out on the streets including perverts masturbating, drunks and desperate homeless people but I always got home safely.

There then followed a number of psychologically disturbing incidents that turned me into an even more withdrawn little girl. I had a chicken and a rabbit as pets and they would run about freely at the end of the garden by a row of bushes. They meant so much to me that I used to rush into the garden to see them the moment I got home. One day, when I was about six years old, I came home from school and walked into the kitchen where my mother was preparing dinner. She was actually cutting the head off a chicken. It was only when I looked out of the window into the garden that I realised my pet chicken was missing. Back in the kitchen, my mother didn't utter a word of explanation as she drained the chicken blood into a pan to start preparing a sauce. I ran out of the kitchen in tears and cried myself to sleep that night.

A few days later, my pet rabbit was killed in similar circumstances and I started to wonder if my mother was doing this deliberately to hurt me. I remember the blood on the white fur and it hanging out drying in the sun. Once again, there was no conversation about why my pets had been slaughtered. When I tried to ask, I was told to stop being so silly. But I've never been able to eat meat since as a result. I never asked my mother why she did it and even now I still don't know if she realised how unhappy she made me feel. I still treasure photos of those two pets today.

I really cannot remember being very close to anyone when I was a child. No one was horrible to me at school, although everyone wore jeans apart from me because my mother always dressed me in brown. I suppose my best friends of all were books. I used to hide under the blankets with a torch most evenings and read late into the night.

Christmas was horrible in our household because everyone shouted and screamed all the time and there were bad arguments between family members. Sometimes, I just wished I could be transported away from this unpleasant environment where love simply wasn't on the agenda. We never went on holidays because we had no money.

I remember one time my mother was away and my father had to do the cooking and we were all teasing him about how bad his food was. He looked heartbroken by our criticism. Suddenly, he grabbed a gun from a drawer, took it out and aimed it at his own head. He then screamed, 'I am going to shoot myself if you keep saying these things.'

As a full-time member of the Communist party staff, he'd been given a gun in case of an uprising. Now he was trying to use it to control me and my baby brother. Looking back on it, it was pathetically dramatic of him. Did he really think we'd be nicer about his food if he pointed a gun at his own head? In some ways, this was the worst form of abuse a child could suffer, because from that day onwards I was constantly worried about my father killing himself.

I remained close to my grandmother throughout my childhood. She was very clever and made more money than anyone else in our family after my bully of a grandfather died when I was still quite young. My mother remained the strict disciplinarian in the family because she'd been so badly beaten by my grandfather. His legacy also meant that she found it virtually impossible to show me any love.

My mother once said to someone that she never had to help me with my homework because I always did it on my own. The truth was that I wanted help but she never offered it. I didn't ask because I was afraid of her shouting at me.

My mother was a controller, which meant, if something didn't happen her way, she became furious. Everything had to be done to her specifications. Naturally, I rebelled against this, although girls do seem to deal with these issues much better than boys do.

I learned to like wine from a very young age because I was often made to step on the grapes in our homemade press in the garden. Legend has it that my great-grandfather would take a big carafe of wine to bed with him every night.

But I felt sorry for my mother. She wanted to laugh but couldn't do it because of what she had suffered in the past. Now I realise she couldn't love anything or anybody. My grandfather's violence towards her made sure of that. My mother let me roam the streets all the time so she could avoid the issue of love. She was always late because she never put herself in my shoes, right back to when she didn't turn up outside kindergarten that time. I always felt sorry for my grandmother because she wanted to love me but my mother wouldn't allow it.

My dreams were always vivid as a child and I remember them all to this day. The most disturbing dream was that my father was standing out on the street exposing his penis. I don't know why I dreamed it but I did. It came over and over again. In real life, he was a good, gentle soul and so that dream hurt me deeply. I always thought my father should be more captivated by my mother and maybe I wanted him to love my mother more.

But there was much worse to come. At home, I began to notice my mother's sister's husband – my uncle – looking at me in a strange way. I didn't think much about it at first. My mother, father, her sister's family and my grandmother were all living under the same roof at the time. My uncle was an important man in the local Communist party and I think all that power went to his head.

One day, he was helping to redecorate the house and I went upstairs to ask him for some paint, which I needed for a school project. I must have been 11 or 12 at the time. He came down off his ladder and told me he'd only give me some paint if I gave him a kiss. I was shocked but allowed him to kiss me on the cheek. Then he tried to put his hands up my skirt. I tried to push him away but he was stronger than me. Then someone came up the stairs and he stopped. I ran away from him but, strangely, I didn't cry. I was just angry with myself for allowing him to do it in the first place. I felt it must have been all my fault. I don't know why I thought like that but I did.

Other times, he just settled for a kiss. I often gave him one to get away. I never told anyone until much later. Why is it that children so often keep the bad stuff to themselves? Isn't it strange the way that, when you are young and something like this happens, you cannot tell anyone? It's almost as if you are afraid to admit what has occurred, even though it is not your own fault.

Some months later, my uncle tried to have actual sex with me. This time, he pushed me against a cupboard in the hallway when everyone else was out of the house. But I was stronger and pushed him off before he could touch me intimately. He was angry with me and didn't seem to understand why I didn't want to have sex with him. It was a lesson to me about the arrogance of men, which I have never forgotten.

Here was my uncle, the big important Communist leader, believing that he had the right to have sex with his 12-year-old niece. How dare he do this? I later found out that he tried to do the same with two of my other female cousins.

When I look back on what happened, I know it has some connection to the fact I was always on my own as a child. Only rarely were adults supervising me and that's why my uncle was able to get away with trying to assault me.

My uncle eventually went after his own daughter, who was around the same age. She was a very attractive girl and when I first told her what her father had done to me she freaked out. Some time later, she came back and told me he had touched her. She even told her mother, whose only response was to tell her not to undress in front of her father. That was it. Obviously, my uncle's behaviour affected my cousin even more than me. She now hates her father and is very distant from all of us.

Another incident occurred to me some time after my uncle's cruel attempts to seduce me. I was a clever but naive teenager so I agreed to let a friend of the family take photos of me in a forest on the outskirts of Budapest. As usual, I had been left to my own devices by my family who didn't seem worried about me going off to the forest with an adult man. I still don't know even today why I went with him.

He pretended he was a professional photographer

but really he was a pervert. Once we got into the middle of the forest, he told me to take off my clothes. I never questioned why. It was almost as if I wanted to please him. I took everything off and then he started taking my picture. Then he started to talk to me in a strange and disgusting manner. That was when I finally knew I was in trouble. I pleaded with him to stop taking the pictures. Trying to grab my clothes back to put them on, I told him how my father and uncle were important members of the Communist party, in the hope that might make him stop. I also said that my father would kill this man if he found out what had happened.

The man was middle-aged and didn't seem bothered by any of my threats. He knew I was trapped with him in the forest. Without his guidance, I'd never find my way out of there. The man then took out a negligee from a bag and ordered me to put it on. 'Then I will lie on you,' he said. I knew then that he intended to have full sex with me. I was terrified. Later on, I decided that his true intention might even have been to kill me.

Then for some reason – I will never know why – I told him I had caught venereal disease from a boyfriend. It worked. He looked appalled and suddenly changed his plans and let me get dressed before we left the forest. This evil character tried to make me feel guilty about not allowing him to have sex. Why was I so naive? Why did I allow him to persuade me to go into the forest with him in the first place? I kept thinking I had let myself down.

I don't remember much more about what happened after we left the forest that day but, as usual, I told no one for years. I should have been able to talk about what happened.

It felt like I'd been travelling on a bus or train and suddenly it had stopped and the landscape wasn't moving any more.

My mother was very closed in. Today, I am a psychologist and I still cannot get close to her. She will not allow it. I don't think my mother and father ever had sex again after my brother's birth. In my twenties, I asked why she didn't leave him and she said he was impotent and she felt so sorry for him.

As a child, my loneliness made me feel very different from everyone else. I often dreamed of being a black woman because they were *really* different. I envied them so much because I wanted to be noticed for all the right reasons.

At the age of 14, I rebelled completely against my parents and cut all my hair off. I looked more like a boy. Then I had eating problems, which were brought on by my low self-esteem. My mother constantly tried to humiliate me. Nothing was ever good enough. She always criticised me. I began to feel I was a bad person destined for an unhappy life.

When I went to my first Catholic confession, I couldn't confess everything bad that I had done because it would have taken too long! And, despite what happened to me when I was younger, I went into the forest many times with boys for sex. I keep wondering why I did that after what I had experienced. I never had that feeling of love from my parents. I kept being told I was not good enough at school. People didn't like me. That's maybe where my amoral attitudes come from.

Even when I got a degree in psychology, my mother wanted me to do something else. 'Why couldn't you have become something normal?' she said to me one day. But then my mother was an obsessive character who could not stop cleaning the house. She never wanted to go out for a meal with me or do anything nice.

Yet, when I was in my mid-teens, my mother suddenly became very overprotective towards me after years of neglect. If she saw a boy looking at me on the bus, she'd get really annoyed.

But then, when I was about 18, she decided that the only way I could progress in life was to marry a rich man. So she sent me to America with just $30 spending money in the hope I would marry a millionaire businessman whom she contacted through a relative. He promised me a life of incredible riches and even said he'd buy me an island off the Bahamas. My mother was desperate for me to do it but I went the other way. I couldn't give my body to this man just because he was rich so I came home determined to be a psychologist.

I have my life completely on track now. In 1986, I obtained an MA in Psychology and after training I moved abroad to learn English. Over the years, I have lived and worked in many different countries. From 1990 to 2000, I worked in private practice as a psychologist and as a relationship and sex therapist.

Between 1994 and 1996, I obtained my MSc in Human Sexuality and gained a diploma in Behaviour and Cognitive Psychotherapy. I was also involved in sex-education programmes in schools. I currently work in private practice at various clinics and I am the mother of a sensible, well-adjusted teenage daughter. I learned from my experiences as a child and can say with complete confidence that everything I went through helped shape my life and I have no regrets.